Beijing

SUMMIT 1

Complete
Assessment Package

with Exam*View*® Software

Joan Saslow ■ Allen Ascher

with Thomas Impola

PEARSON
Longman

Summit: English for Today's World   1
Complete Assessment Package

with **ExamView** *Assessment Suite* CD-ROM

Pearson Education, 10 Bank Street, White Plains, NY 10606

Staff credits: The people who made up the *Summit 1 Complete Assessment Package* team— representing editorial, production, design, manufacturing, and multimedia—are Rhea Banker, Dave Dickey, Pamela Fishman, Ann France, Aliza Greenblatt, Caroline Kasterine, Mike Kemper, Sasha Kintzler, and Siobhan Sullivan.

ISBN: 0-13-110633-3

Illustration credits: Leanne Franson: Unit 4, p. 2, Unit 9, p. 4; Philippe Germain: Unit 3, p. 3; Stephen Hutchings: Review Test 2, p. 6; Suzanne Mogensen: Unit 2, p. 2, Unit 8, p. 3; Steve Schulman: Unit 4, p. 3, Unit 6, p. 4.

Photo credits: Unit 2, p. 3: Bruno Vincent/Getty Images; Review Test 1, p. 6: Bettman/Corbis; Unit 7, p. 4: Royalty-Free/Corbis.

Printed in the United States of America
3 4 5 6 7 8 9 10—CRS—11 10 09 08 07

The *Summit 1 Complete Assessment Package* contains the following photocopiable tests for the *Summit 1* Student's Book:

- An Achievement Test for each of the ten units
- Review Test 1 for Units 1–5
- Writing Test 1 for Units 1–5
- Speaking Test 1 for Units 1–5
- Review Test 2 for Units 6–10
- Writing Test 2 for Units 6–10
- Speaking Test 2 for Units 6–10

Also included with the tests are:

- The audio CD with the listening comprehension tracks
- The audioscript to accompany the audio CD
- The answer key
- The Exam*View*® CD-ROM which allows you to customize the tests (See pages vi–ix for further explanation.)

ACHIEVEMENT TESTS

The Achievement Tests offer the opportunity to evaluate students' progress on a unit-by-unit basis. Each of the ten Achievement Tests is designed to be given upon completion of the corresponding unit in the Student's Book. Each Achievement Test contains 33 items and evaluates students' progress in the following skills:

- Listening
- Vocabulary and social language
- Grammar
- Reading
- Writing

REVIEW TESTS

Similar to the Achievement Tests, the two Review Tests evaluate students' progress in the above-mentioned skills. Their purpose is to provide cumulative assessment. Review Test 1 is designed to be given after Units 1–5 and Review Test 2 after Units 6–10. Each Review Test contains 60 items targeting the language taught in the corresponding five units of the Student's Book.

WRITING TESTS

The two Writing Tests provide additional cumulative assessment. Writing Test 1 is designed to be given after Units 1–5 and Writing Test 2 after Units 6–10. Each Writing Test contains two topics for students to choose from. The topics are designed to encourage students to use the language taught in the corresponding five units.

SPEAKING TESTS

The two Speaking Tests also provide additional cumulative assessment. Speaking Test 1 is designed to be given after Units 1–5 and Speaking Test 2 after Units 6–10. Each Speaking Test contains three topics for students to choose from. The topics are designed to encourage students to use the language taught in the corresponding five units.

ADMINISTERING THE TESTS

ACHIEVEMENT TESTS AND REVIEW TESTS   Each Achievement Test, including the listening comprehension section, is designed to take approximately 25 to 30 minutes to administer. Each Review Test, including the listening comprehension section, requires approximately 50 minutes. Teachers may allow more or less time for any given test, depending on the needs of their students, without affecting the validity of the test.

The tests are designed with the assumption that the listening comprehension section will be administered at the beginning of each test. This way the listening comprehension section can be administered to all students at the same time without interfering with the other parts of the test. Play the audio CD and have students listen and answer the questions. Each listening exercise is recorded twice.

WRITING TESTS   The Writing Tests are designed to be conducted immediately after the Review Tests or at a separate time. Give students at least 5 minutes to choose the topic they will write about. Then give students 30 minutes to write their essays.

SPEAKING TESTS   The Speaking Tests are designed to be conducted separately from the Review Tests. Make sure students have ample time to choose their topics and prepare before they present.

SCORING THE TESTS

ACHIEVEMENT TESTS   Each Achievement Test consists of 33 items. To get a percentage score, multiply the number of correct items by 3 and add 1 "free" point.

REVIEW TESTS   Each Review Test consists of 60 items worth 1.25 points each for a total of 75 points.

WRITING TESTS   Each Writing Test is worth 15 points.

SPEAKING TESTS   Each Speaking Test is worth 10 points.

The Review Test, Writing Test, and Speaking Test together are worth a total of 100 points. To get a percentage score, multiply the number of correct items on the Review Test by 1.25 and then add this to the points earned on the Writing Test and the points earned on the Speaking Test.

SCORING RUBRICS FOR WRITING AND SPEAKING

ACHIEVEMENT TESTS AND REVIEW TESTS   When evaluating student writing skills on the essay sections of the Achievement and Review Tests, take the following criteria equally into account.

Appropriateness:	Essay is on topic.
Completeness:	Essay has a suitable amount of detail and addresses all aspects of the given topic.
Accuracy:	Sentences are correct in terms of grammar, spelling, and punctuation; vocabulary and social language expressions are used appropriately.

On the Achievement Tests, where the essay sections are worth 9 points each, give students up to 3 points for each criterion. Each essay question on the Review Tests is worth a total of 3.75 points. Give students up to 1.25 points for each criterion. There are sample responses for each writing topic in the answer key.

WRITING TESTS   When evaluating student writing skills on the Writing Tests, take the following criteria equally into account.

Appropriateness:	Essay is on topic.
Completeness:	Essay contains at least three paragraphs and addresses all aspects of the given topic.
Accuracy:	Sentences are correct in terms of grammar, spelling, and punctuation; vocabulary and social language expressions are used appropriately.
Clarity:	Essay is well organized; ideas are presented in a clear and logical manner; details are used to clarify and illustrate ideas.
Complexity:	Essay contains a variety of sentence structures and tenses; vocabulary is varied.

Give students up to 3 points for each criterion.

SPEAKING TESTS   When evaluating student speaking skills on the Speaking Tests, take the following criteria equally into account.

Appropriateness:	Talk is on topic.
Completeness:	Talk addresses all aspects of the given topic.
Accuracy:	Speech is grammatically correct; vocabulary and social language expressions are used appropriately.
Fluency:	Speech flows smoothly and is not halting; the student speaks with ease and confidence.
Intelligibility:	Speech is clear and could be readily understood by a native speaker.

Give students up to 2 points for each criterion.

WHAT IS Exam*View*®?

Exam*View*® *Assessment Suite 5.0* is a test-generator program that allows you to easily create and customize tests. With this program, you can organize test questions any way you want. You can delete questions, edit questions, or add new questions. You can scramble questions and / or answer choices to create different versions of a single test. The program automatically creates answer keys for each test you create with it. Exam*View* also allows you to customize the appearance of the tests you create. It comes with a sophisticated word processor and allows numerous layout and printing options. You can use Exam*View* to create printed tests, Internet tests, or tests that could be placed on a local area network (LAN) and administered in a computer lab.

The Exam*View Assessment Suite* is comprised of the Test Generator, Test Player, and Test Manager. The Test Generator is used to create assessment items, study guides, and tests. The Test Player is used by students to take tests that have been placed on a local area network (LAN). The Test Manager is used to view reports of test results.

SUMMIT AND Exam*View*®

Exam*View* organizes questions by question bank. A question bank is a group of questions. The Exam*View* CD-ROM in this book comes with pre-filled question banks for *Summit 1*. Each question bank on this CD-ROM corresponds to one of the photocopiable tests in this book. You can add or remove questions from a question bank, edit the questions within a question bank, or even create new question banks.

In order to provide you with greater flexibility and convenience, extra questions have been provided in each question bank in addition to the questions in the photocopiable tests in this book. You can use these extra questions in addition to the other test questions or as alternates for them.

In addition to being categorized by question bank, each question in Exam*View* is labeled by skill, objective, and difficulty. Skill refers to the skills evaluated in *Summit* which are: listening; vocabulary and social language; grammar; reading; and writing. Objective refers to specific learning objectives and corresponds to the social language, vocabulary, and grammar topics from *Summit 1*. Difficulty is described on a scale of 1–3, where level 1 is easy, level 2 is moderately challenging, and level 3 is difficult. The *Summit* photocopiable tests were designed to have the following distribution of difficulty: 80% difficulty level 1; 10% difficulty level 2; and 10% difficulty level 3. In *Summit,* difficulty 1 questions include all objective questions such as multiple choice and true / false items; difficulty 2 questions include all items that require students to write a free-response sentence; and difficulty 3 questions include all short essay questions where students are asked to write a paragraph.

HOW TO CREATE TESTS WITH Exam*View*®

There are many different ways to create tests, using Exam*View*. Generally, the first step will be to select the question bank or banks you want to use. Next, select the questions you want to include. This can be done in a few different ways. You can choose to view all the test questions in the selected question bank or banks and then choose questions individually. Or you can choose questions without viewing them, simply based on criteria such as: skill; objective; difficulty; or question type (multiple choice, true / false, short answer, etc.). Specify the number of questions you'd like and the program will generate a test by randomly choosing from the questions that match the criteria you've selected. Once you've chosen your questions you can edit them if necessary.

SYSTEM REQUIREMENTS

To use the Exam*View*® *Assessment Suite* v.5.0, your computer must meet or exceed the following requirements:

WINDOWS®

- PC with Pentium II 120 MHz or higher processor
- Microsoft Windows 98 or later operating system
- 32 MB available memory for application (64 MB recommended)
- 24 MB of available hard drive space

MACINTOSH®

- PowerPC 120 MHz or higher processor
- OS X 10.2 or later operating system
- 32 MB available memory for application (64 MB recommended)
- 24 MB of available hard drive space

INSTALLING Exam*View*®

Follow these steps to install the Exam*View Assessment Suite* on your hard drive.

WINDOWS®

- Insert the Exam*View* disc into the CD-ROM drive.

- Click the **Start** button on the task bar and choose the *Run* option.

- Type **d:\setup.exe** (where **d** is the letter of your CD-ROM drive) and press **Enter**.

- Follow the prompts on the screen to complete the installation process.

- Remove the disc from the CD-ROM drive when you have finished.

MACINTOSH®

- Insert the Exam*View* disc into your CD-ROM drive.

- Open the installer window, if necessary.

- Double-click the installation icon to start the program.

- Follow the prompts on the screen to complete the installation process.

- Remove the disc from the CD-ROM drive when you have finished.

After you have completed the installation process, follow these instructions to start the Exam*View* test-generator software.

Windows: Click the **Exam*View* Test Generator** shortcut on your desktop. If you do not have a shortcut, click the **Start** button. Highlight the **Programs** menu and locate the **Exam*View* Pro Test Generator** folder. Select the **Exam*View* Test Generator** option.

Macintosh: Click the **Exam*View* Test Generator** icon on your dock. If you do not see this icon, locate the **Exam*View* Pro** folder on your hard drive. Double-click the **Exam*View* Test Generator** icon.

The first time you run the software, you will be prompted to enter your name, school / institution name, and city / state. You are now ready to begin using the Exam*View* software.

PRODUCT SUPPORT

Whenever you need assistance using Exam*View*, access the extensive help system. Click the **Help** button and choose an option from the **Help** menu to access step-by-step instructions from more than 150 help topics. If you experience any difficulties while you are working with the software, you may want to review the troubleshooting tips in the user-friendly help system.

TECHNICAL SUPPORT

For technical support worldwide, e-mail EPSupport@pearsoned.com or call us. Within the United States, dial 1-877-546-5408. Outside the United States, dial +1-914-287-8087.

Our technical staff will need to know certain things about your system in order to help us solve your problems more quickly and efficiently. If possible, please be at your computer when you call for support. You should have the following information ready:

- product title and product ISBN
- computer make and model
- RAM available
- hard disk space available
- graphics card type
- printer make and model (if applicable)
- detailed description of the problem, including the exact wording of any error messages

Name _____

🎧 **Listen to each conversation. Read the sentences. Then listen again and check <u>true</u> or <u>false</u>.**

Conversation A

		true	false
Example:	Carla and Dan are planning a business meeting.	☐	☑
1.	Dan is a workaholic.	☐	☐
2.	Dan thinks that his boss is a tyrant.	☐	☐

Conversation B

3.	Dan thinks that his co-worker, Harry, is a team player.	☐	☐
4.	According to Dan, Harry is not a people person.	☐	☐

Conversation C

5.	Carla thinks that her neighbor, John, is a sweetheart.	☐	☐
6.	In Carla's opinion, John is a wise guy.	☐	☐

Complete each sentence with a word or phrase from the box. You will not use all of the words.

~~team player~~	tyrant
people person	workaholic
brain	wise guy

Example: Camille always works well with others, and her group is always successful. Camille is a _team player_ .

7. Claire is always working, even at home. She never spends time relaxing with friends or family. Claire is a _____ .

8. Mark is really friendly and kind to everyone. Everyone loves him. Mark is a

_____ .

9. June learns very quickly and seems to know everything about everything. June is a

_____ .

Classify the following adjectives as <u>positive</u> or <u>negative</u>. Circle the correct answer.

Example:	impolite	positive	(negative)
10.	helpful	positive	negative
11.	reliable	positive	negative
12.	offensive	positive	negative
13.	annoying	positive	negative

Circle the word or phrase that correctly completes each sentence.

Example: "The travel agent is going to call and leave a message about our flight, so don't forget (to listen) / **listening** to your messages when you get home."

14. "Tomorrow is our anniversary—did you remember **to ask / asking** your boss for the afternoon off?"

15. "I'll never forget **to hear / hearing** the sound of wolves howling at the moon when we were on our trip in Alaska."

16. "I didn't expect **to like / liking** her so much, but I really do."

Complete each sentence with the correct form of the verb in parentheses.

Example: "We need some milk and butter. Don't forget _to stop_ at the store on your
way home."
(stop)

17. "Edgar introduced us at a party, and it was very embarrassing. She obviously knew me, but
I didn't remember _____ her."
(meet)

18. "Oh no! I forgot _____ the garbage out! It'll have to wait until
(take)
Wednesday."

19. "It's getting late. Let's not stop _____—we can have dinner when we
(eat)
get home."

20. "Alice is so beautiful—I will never forget _____ her for the first time."
(see)

21. "Do you remember _____ for a pay raise? Well, it looks like you're going
(ask)
to get one!"

Read the message board. Then read it again and check the correct sentence.

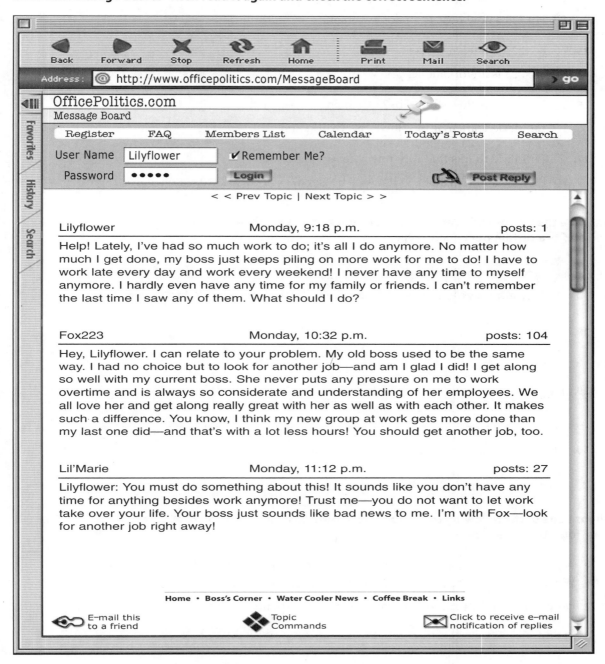

OfficePolitics.com
Message Board

Register   FAQ   Members List   Calendar   Today's Posts   Search

User Name Lilyflower   ☑ Remember Me?
Password ••••• Login   Post Reply

< < Prev Topic | Next Topic > >

Lilyflower   Monday, 9:18 p.m.   posts: 1

Help! Lately, I've had so much work to do; it's all I do anymore. No matter how much I get done, my boss just keeps piling on more work for me to do! I have to work late every day and work every weekend! I never have any time to myself anymore. I hardly even have any time for my family or friends. I can't remember the last time I saw any of them. What should I do?

Fox223   Monday, 10:32 p.m.   posts: 104

Hey, Lilyflower. I can relate to your problem. My old boss used to be the same way. I had no choice but to look for another job—and am I glad I did! I get along so well with my current boss. She never puts any pressure on me to work overtime and is always so considerate and understanding of her employees. We all love her and get along really great with her as well as with each other. It makes such a difference. You know, I think my new group at work gets more done than my last one did—and that's with a lot less hours! You should get another job, too.

Lil'Marie   Monday, 11:12 p.m.   posts: 27

Lilyflower: You must do something about this! It sounds like you don't have any time for anything besides work anymore! Trust me—you do not want to let work take over your life. Your boss just sounds like bad news to me. I'm with Fox—look for another job right away!

Home • Boss's Corner • Water Cooler News • Coffee Break • Links

E-mail this to a friend   Topic Commands   Click to receive e-mail notification of replies

---

Example: ☑ Lilyflower thinks her boss is bad news.

☐ Lilyflower thinks her boss is likable and easy to get along with.

22. ☐ Lilyflower thinks that her boss is a brain.

☐ Lilyflower thinks her boss is a tyrant.

23. ☐ Fox223's new boss is a pain in the neck.

☐ Fox223's new boss is a sweetheart.

24.   ☐ Fox223's old boss is a people person.

   ☐ Fox223's new boss is a people person.

25.   ☐ Fox223 is a team player.

   ☐ Fox223 is a workaholic.

26.   ☐ Lil'Marie believes that Fox223 is being a wise guy.

   ☐ Lil'Marie fears that Lilyflower is a workaholic.

27.   ☐ Lil'Marie thinks that Lilyflower complains a lot.

   ☐ Lil'Marie thinks that Lilyflower's boss makes her work extremely hard.

Describe the personalities of some people you know. Explain how each person fits a certain personality type.

Example: My _classmate, Julie,_ is such a _brain_ .
She always knows all the answers to our teacher's questions .

28.   My _____ is a real _____ .

   _____ .

29.   Her _____ is such a _____ .

   _____ .

30.   Our _____ is a real _____ .

   _____ .

Choose one of the following topics to write about. Write a paragraph of at least four to five sentences.

• A pessimist says, "The glass is half empty." An optimist says, "The glass is half full." What are some of the pros and cons of each perspective?

• Do you find it difficult to find balance in life? Explain.

31–33.   _____

_____

_____

_____

_____

_____

Name _____

🎧 **Listen to the conversation. Read the sentences. Then listen again and circle the word or phrase that correctly completes each sentence.**

| **Example:** | Sharon thinks new age music is **exciting** / (**annoying.**) |

1. Theresa **is passionate about / does not like** George Winston's music.

2. For Sharon, the new age sound is **depressing / boring**.

3. Sharon likes the beat of **George Winston's / Beyoncé's** music.

4. Sharon likes to be **excited / relaxed** by music.

5. **Sharon / Theresa** likes mellow beats and gentle melodies.

6. **Dennis / Theresa** has an extra ticket to see Beyoncé.

Circle the letter of the answer that correctly completes each sentence.

| **Example:** | "Keith always likes to keep busy with several projects and activities—both at work and at home. He's very _____." |
| | **a.** egotistical   (**b.**) energetic   **c.** passionate |

7. "Jeff will only work on projects that he feels very strongly about, and once he begins on one, he becomes very dedicated to it. He is a very _____ man."

   a. moody   **b.** passionate   **c.** eccentric

8. "Jessica always has interesting ideas that no one else has thought of. She is extremely _____."

   a. eccentric   **b.** difficult   **c.** imaginative

9. "Alice plays the piano beautifully. She always has—even before she had her first lesson. She is just naturally _____."

   a. gifted   **b.** difficult   **c.** moody

10. "You never know what Laura is thinking. She can be very pleasant one moment and very unpleasant the next. She's so _____."

    a. moody   **b.** egotistical   **c.** passionate

11. "It seems that Eric just likes to argue about everything. I've never met anyone so _____."

    a. egotistical   **b.** eccentric   **c.** difficult

Look at each picture. Complete each sentence with the correct form of the verb in parentheses.

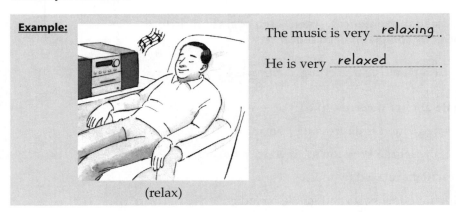

Example:

The music is very _relaxing_.

He is very _relaxed_.

(relax)

(annoy)

(depress)

12. She is _____.

The fly is _____.

13. She is _____.

The book is _____.

(bore)

(excite)

14. The concert is _____.

The audience is _____.

15. The show is _____.

The audience is _____.

Read the magazine article. Then read it again and check <u>true</u> or <u>false</u>.

Youssou N'Dour
Brilliant West African Musician

N'Dour's music creates a new and exciting sound.

One of the most popular African singers of recent decades, Youssou N'Dour has been responsible for bringing the music of his native Senegal to a wider audience. N'Dour belongs to the West African tradition of *griots*, oral historians who tell stories over musical beats. Growing up with the songs and stories of West Africa, and influenced by Cuban jazz and American R&B and pop, N'Dour developed a style of music known as *mbalax*. This unique style mixes together these traditional and Western influences to create a new and exciting sound.

N'Dour sings in English, French, and several West African languages. His expressive, five-octave tenor has been heralded as one of the finest voices in the world. *Rolling Stone* magazine once described N'Dour as "a singer with a voice so extraordinary that the history of Africa seems locked inside it." With a characteristic mix of the old and new, N'Dour's songwriting contains themes from West African fables as well as commentary on modern social and environmental issues.

N'Dour's band, the Étoile de Dakar, plays both West African and Western instruments. The *tama* and *sabar*, traditional Senegalese drums, blend with electric guitar, keyboard, and saxophone to create a complex, energetic dance rhythm. Traditional stringed instruments like the *kora*, *xalam*, and *riti* add folk melodies into the mix. Collaborations with artists such as Peter Gabriel, Sting, Neneh Cherry, and Branford Marsalis have brought Youssou N'Dour to a worldwide audience, with the beauty and power of his music breaking down language and culture barriers. He is West Africa's first international superstar.

Source: www.allmusic.com

		true	false
Example:	The article is a description of an African musician.	☑	☐
16.	The main focus of the article is the singer's personality type.	☐	☐
17.	Youssou N'Dour's most popular song is called <u>mbalax</u>.	☐	☐
18.	N'Dour's sound is a mix of African and Western music.	☐	☐
19.	N'Dour's lyrics comment on modern and traditional themes.	☐	☐
20.	The <u>xalam</u> is a type of traditional African folk melody.	☐	☐
21.	N'Dour's voice has impressed music critics.	☐	☐
22.	N'Dour's songs have strong beats that are created using traditional West African drums.	☐	☐

Complete each sentence with either the simple past tense, the present perfect, or the present perfect continuous form of the verb in parentheses. Use the present perfect continuous if the action is unfinished or ongoing.

> **Example:** "James couldn't believe I had never been to a jazz club, so we ___went___ to one last week."
> (go)

23. "Isn't he a great piano player? He _____ at this club since it first opened."
(play)

24. "I hear that you're a big James Brown fan. How many times _____ him?"
(see)

25. "I had never heard Caetano Veloso before. I loved the show, so I went right out and _____ three of his CDs."
(buy)

26. "Wow! Your singing sounds great now! I can tell that you _____."
(practice)

27. "_____ any good new music lately?"
(hear)

Complete each sentence in your own way. Use noun clauses.

> **Example:** **A:** What should I bring on vacation with me?
> **B:** You should bring _whatever you want to bring_.

28. **A:** What do you like most about being a musician?
    B: I love the fact _____.

29. **A:** What did your sister want to know?
    B: She wanted to know _____.

30. **A:** How do you think music influences people?
    B: It's my opinion _____.

Choose one of the following topics to write about. Write a paragraph of at least four to five sentences.

- Describe your favorite type of music in terms of beat, melody, and lyrics.
- Who is the most musically talented person you know? Describe that person's personality, abilities, and accomplishments.

31–33. _____

_____

_____

_____

_____

Name _____

🎧 **Listen to the conversation. Read the sentences. Then listen again and check true or false.**

	true	false
Example: The man and woman are talking about financial goals.	☑	☐
1. The woman has clear long-term financial goals.	☐	☐
2. The man did not expect to have such a serious conversation.	☐	☐
3. The man and woman are both over 40.	☐	☐
4. The woman plans to retire at 40.	☐	☐
5. The woman plans to be financially secure by the time she is 40.	☐	☐
6. The woman knew that the man was going to pay for dinner.	☐	☐

Circle the letter of the answer that correctly completes each sentence.

Example: "Jim will spend two hours looking for a restaurant that gives free bread. I can't believe he is _____."

    (a.) so cheap   **b.** so generous   **c.** such a spendthrift

7. "It's not hard to be _____; you just have to spend a little less and save a little more."

    a. thrifty   **b.** stingy   **c.** a spendthrift

8. "Whenever Jeremiah goes into a record store, he comes out with four or five CDs for himself. He's _____."

    a. a real tightwad   **b.** a real spendthrift   **c.** really generous

9. "My uncle is so _____ he won't even buy ice cream for his own children."

    a. generous   **b.** frugal   **c.** stingy

10. "Jeanne always shares whatever she has with everyone. She's the most _____ person I know."

    a. frugal   **b.** stingy   **c.** generous

11. "They are all saying I'm a _____ just because I said that I would rather walk than pay for parking."

    a. tightwad   **b.** big spender   **c.** spendthrift

Complete each sentence with a word from the box. You will not use all of the words.

money	philanthropist	contribution	charity
investment	profit	~~donations~~	

Example: "Charitable *donations* _____ usually increase around the holidays."

12. "Some people give 10 percent of their money to a favorite _____ *ch* or not-for-profit organization."

13. "Would you like to make a _____ *con* to help fight childhood diseases?"

14. "If we buy roses for £1.00 and sell them for £2.00, we'll make a 100 percent _____ *profit*."

Rewrite each sentence, using the past unreal conditional: inverted form.

Example: "If we had been told it would cost so much to maintain, we never would have bought this car."

Had we been told this car would cost so much to maintain, we never would have bought it.

15. "If I had known this furniture would be so hard to put together, I wouldn't have bought it."

Had I known

16. "We would've bought a smaller couch if we had realized this one wouldn't fit in the elevator."

Had we realized this could

17. "If he had known his digital camera would just sit around collecting dust, he wouldn't have bought such an expensive one."

Had he known (wouldn't)

Complete each sentence in your own way. Write about your financial plans or goals for the future.

Example: By the end of the summer, I expect *to have saved enough money to buy a new car*.

18. By the time _____, I hope _____.

19. I plan _____ by the end of next month.

20. By this time next year, I _____.

Read the magazine article. Then read it again and circle the word or phrase that correctly completes each sentence.

A gift-giver's guide
Things to consider when choosing a gift

You've experienced buyer's remorse—that feeling of regret that comes from buying something you didn't really need or shouldn't have bought. And you may have even experienced a bit of "receiver's remorse," too—the disappointment of opening up a beautifully wrapped gift to discover—oh, dear—something you don't need that someone else shouldn't have bought. Here's a gift-buyer's guide for avoiding buyer's (and receiver's) remorse.

Hidden costs
When choosing a gift, be mindful that the store price tag may not be the only cost. Some products require regular  service or care to keep them operational. My grandmother once received a large tropical fish aquarium as a gift. However, the aquarium used so much electricity that her electric bill doubled.

Space issues
Here's something else to think about: size. Sure, my sister would love an exercise bike, but would it fit in her tiny studio apartment? When purchasing large or bulky items, think about where they are going to be kept. Is there enough space? Where will it be stored when not in use?

Size of the manual
Everybody loves technology, but before buying that new gadget, measure the thickness of the instruction manual. Will the person need an engineering degree just to figure out how to use it? I once bought a digital camera for my uncle. A year later, when I noticed him still taking pictures with  his old camera, I asked about the digital camera. He admitted that he had returned it after failing to find the power button.

Some assembly required
Two important rules when choosing a gift that the receivers must put together themselves: 1) They shouldn't need to use more than two tools; 2) The product must not come in more than six pieces. My daughter was given a wagon that took me over four hours to put together. I cut my hand using the wrong screwdriver, and I never could get the wheels to spin correctly. I hate that wagon.

Practicality
Finally, it's important to consider how practical the gift is  for the person receiving it. Let's face it, it could be a great product, but it's only a great gift if it gets used. I bought my brother one of those big electric mixers just because it looked cool. Since he doesn't cook, however, it never left his kitchen cabinet.

Example: The article ⟨offers shopping advice⟩ / recommends places to shop.

21. The article is written for people who **buy gifts / receive gifts**.

22. The article offers advice on how to avoid **spending too much money / buyer's remorse**.

23. The author's grandmother was given an aquarium that **cost too much to maintain / was too hard to operate**.

24. An exercise bike would be a poor choice for the author's sister because it would **just sit around collecting dust / take up so much room**.

25. The author's uncle returned the digital camera because it was so hard to **operate / put together**.

26. The author dislikes the wagon because it was hard to **put together / operate**.

27. An electric mixer wasn't a good gift for the author's brother because it **just sits around collecting dust / costs so much to maintain**.

Match each sentence beginning to the correct ending. You will not use all of the sentence endings.

Example: "There's always something with this computer that needs to be fixed or updated. I would've bought a different brand had I known this one would _____d_____."

28. "I would have bought already-assembled furniture had I known this do-it-yourself kind would _____c_____."

29. "I wouldn't have bought this confusing, high-tech camcorder had I known it would _____b_____."

30. "I wouldn't have gotten this big exercise machine that doesn't fit in any of my closets had I known it would _____."

a. take up so much room
b. be so hard to operate
c. be so hard to put together
d. cost so much to maintain
e. just sit around collecting dust

Choose one of the following topics to write about. Write a paragraph of at least four to five sentences.

• What are your short-term financial goals? Refer to specific completion dates.

• Have you had any experiences with charitable organizations? What kinds of groups will you give (or not give) your money to in the future?

31–33. _____

_____

_____

_____

_____

Name _____

🎧 **Listen to the conversation. Read the sentences. Then listen again and check the correct sentence.**

> **Example:** ☐ Margaret has just had her hair done.
> ☑ Paul has just had his hair done.

1. ☐ The majority of Paul's friends think his haircut is too flashy.
   ☐ A few of Paul's friends think his haircut is too flashy.

2. ☐ Margaret thinks buzz cuts are out of style.
   ☐ Margaret thinks buzz cuts are hot right now.

3. ☐ Margaret thinks Paul's hair color might be offensive to some people.
   ☐ Margaret thinks Paul's hair color is chic.

4. ☐ Margaret thinks most bank employees dress in a classic way.
   ☐ Margaret thinks most bank employees wear trendy clothes to work.

5. ☐ Paul wears trendy clothes to work.
   ☐ Paul wears formal business clothes to work.

6. ☐ Margaret thinks most bank customers don't trust bank employees who dress in a classic style.
   ☐ Margaret thinks most bank customers don't trust bank employees who dress in a shocking way.

Complete each sentence with a word from the box. You will not use all of the words.

centered	confident	~~confidence~~	esteem
image	pity	conscious	critical

> **Example:** "I wish I had more self-_confidence_; then I wouldn't be so nervous when I met new people."

7. "A positive self-_____ is the result of feeling good about the way you look, feel, and act."

8. "Don't be so self-_____. Nobody really cares what you're wearing."

9. "I think that James wears all those flashy clothes because he wants to be accepted. I'm afraid he has low self-_____."

10. "People who are quick to indulge in self-_____ are also quick to lose friends; they always feel sorry for themselves and aren't much fun to be around."

Look at each picture. Circle the letter of the answer that correctly completes each sentence.

Example:

"He has _____ look."

a. an elegant

b. an old-fashioned

c. a shocking

11. "Those boots are so _____ right now."

a. out of style

b. hot

c. flashy

12. "Look at what he's wearing! I'm sorry, but that's just _____."

a. tacky

b. chic

c. elegant

13. "Don't they look _____!"

a. tacky

b. shocking

c. elegant

14. "She looks so _____. That look was hot three years ago!"

a. out of style

b. fashionable

c. chic

**Read the magazine article. Then read it again and circle the letter of the
answer that correctly completes each sentence.**

From Shocking to Striking

Tattoos Gain Acceptance

Just as fashions come and go, standards for appropriate dress continue to change. This change is often accepted by some sooner than others. What is attractive or trendy in one situation may be seen as shocking or tacky in another. In Western society, tattoos are an example of this.

Fifty years ago, a tattoo was a symbol of nonconformity. A person with a tattoo was seen as devious and offensive. This began to change in the 1960s, as many standards for dress, grooming, and behavior began to change. Rock 'n' roll musicians were among the first to wear tattoos as a way to rebel against society's rules. Eventually, athletes, models, and movie stars also began to wear tattoos.

Today, tattoos are seen on all types of people. For many teenagers, tattoos are an expression of individuality and self-confidence. Smaller, more subdued tattoos are hardly even noticed.

It is too early to say that tattoos have achieved total social acceptance. A tattoo could still be a "career-killer" in more conservative professions such as banking or finance. However, plenty of people are now entering the business world with tattoos they got as students. Eventually, these people will become business leaders, and the style will be more acceptable. When we see a tattoo on a president or prime minister, we will know that tattoos have finally arrived.

Example: According to the first paragraph, _____.

    a. tattoos are in bad taste

    b. tattoos are both elegant and classic

    c. tattoos are accepted by some but not by others

15. Before the 1960s, people with tattoos were _____.

    a. in style

    b. shocking

    c. respectable

16. Rock 'n' roll musicians began to wear tattoos because _____.

    a. they wanted to show that they didn't follow society's rules

    b. they wanted to be part of society

    c. they wanted to be trendy

17. In the 1960s, _____.

    a. models had tattoos but rock musicians did not

    b. tattoos gradually started to become stylish

    c. tattoos were still not accepted by anyone

18. According to the article, _____.

    a. some teenagers see tattoos as a symbol of their individuality

    b. teenagers are self-conscious

    c. a majority of teenagers are afraid to be seen as self-confident

19. According to the last paragraph, _____.

    a. most students with tattoos go into the business world

    b. visible tattoos could still be a problem in some professions

    c. tattoos have already achieved total social acceptance

20. The main idea of this article is that _____.

    a. tattoos are losing popularity

    b. tattoos are now acceptable to everyone

    c. tattoos are more acceptable now than before

Complete each sentence in your own way. Write sentences about fashion or style.

Example: A few *managers in my company don't like casual Fridays* .

21. A majority of _____.

22. Most _____.

23. Several _____.

Circle the word or phrase that correctly completes each sentence.

> **Example:**   Models have (no)/ **many** / **few** choice at fashion shows; they have to wear what the designers tell them to wear.

24. When it comes to business clothes, **no / most / a little** conformity is better than none.

25. **The majority / Several / A few** of the group thinks that it's not acceptable to wear bathing suits to that restaurant.

26. Some managers worry that "casual Friday" means **few / less / a number of** productivity.

27. It seems that now more than ever, **every / most / much** teenagers dress to impress their friends and classmates.

28. **Many / A great deal of / Not as much** designers focus on casual clothing.

29. The new dress code has been met with **several / a great deal of / many** satisfaction.

30. **Only a few / Not as much / Less** managers object to casual clothing in the office.

Choose one of the following topics to write about. Write a paragraph of at least four to five sentences. Use some of the words from the box.

- Compare the clothes you wear when you are at work or school to the ones you wear when you are out with friends or at home. Are they different?

- Think of a style that you would never wear. Compare it to a style that you usually wear. Explain.

like	but	similarly
however	too / also	whereas / while

31–33. ....

....

....

....

....

UNIT 5 ■ Achievement Test

Name _____

🎧 Listen to the conversation. Read the sentences. Then listen again and check
true or **false**.

	true	false
Example: Sandra is planning a trip to the city.	☐	☑
1. Matt thinks people's behavior in the city is unacceptable at times.	☐	☐
2. It really bugs Sandra when people bump into her on the street.	☐	☐
3. Matt thinks city people are impolite and discourteous.	☐	☐
4. Matt thinks it is inconsiderate when people litter.	☐	☐
5. Matt does not mind when people talk loudly on their cell phones.	☐	☐

Write the antonym of each adjective below. Use the negative prefixes from the box.

dis-	im-	in-	ir-	un-

Example: polite ≠ _impolite_

6. acceptable ≠ _____

7. proper ≠ _____

8. honest ≠ _____

9. excusable ≠ _____

10. rational ≠ _____

Complete each sentence with a word or phrase from the box. Make changes as necessary.

~~beautify your town~~	donate your organs	clean up litter	volunteer

Example: " _Beautify your town_ by planting trees or flowers where there are none."

11. "Mike _____ at a hospital. He doesn't get paid for his work; he does it because community service is important to him."

12. "Have you ever considered _____ so that you could save the lives of others after you die?"

13. "It's important not to leave any trash behind and to _____ left lying around."

Complete each sentence in your own way. Use possessives with gerunds.

Example: _My husband's smoking_ really bothers me.

14. _____ really ticks me off.

15. _____ gets on my nerves.

16. _____ really bugs me.

1

Combine each pair of sentences into one new sentence. Use a possessive with a gerund.

> **Example:**   They laughed during the wedding. I didn't like it.
>
> _I didn't like their laughing during the wedding._

17. Jacob moved out of the city. He says that it is the best thing he has ever done for himself.

    ....

18. Maria smokes. Her boyfriend is getting worried about it.

    ....

19. They argue. I think it's getting worse and worse.

    ....

20. Chris talks on his cell phone during meetings. His boss is really getting annoyed by it.

    ....

Combine each pair of sentences into one new sentence. Use the words in the box.

either . . . or	neither . . . nor	not only . . . but also

> **Example:**   You may smoke in the lounge. You may smoke outside.
>
> _You may smoke either in the lounge or outside._

21. Driving in the city is not convenient. Driving in the city is not enjoyable.

    ....

22. You can help your community by volunteering your time. If you are too busy, you can donate money.

    ....

23. Smoke-filled rooms are unpleasant. Smoke-filled rooms are unhealthy.

    ....

24. The traffic was terrible. The weather was awful.

    ....

Read the article. Then read it again and circle the letter of the correct answer.

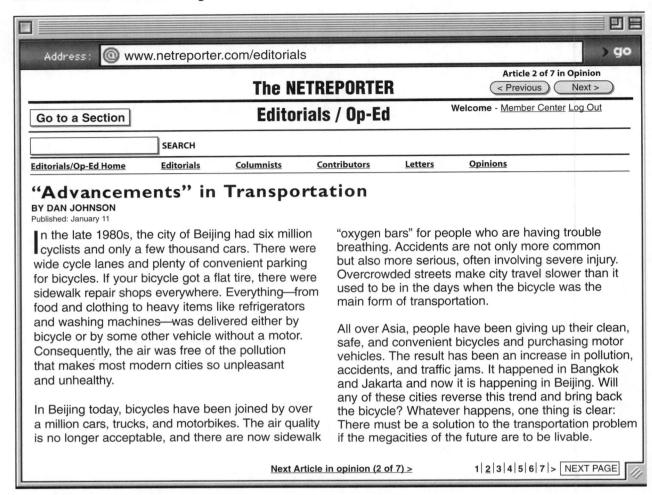

Example: Which of the following is a main idea of this article?

   a. Transportation in megacities is improving.

   b. It is difficult to cure breathing problems.

   c. Bicycles are not only convenient but also safe.

25. Which statement is true, according to the first paragraph?

   a. Not only food and clothing but also heavy items such as washing machines were delivered by bicycle in Beijing.

   b. Heavy items must be delivered by vehicles with motors.

   c. Motor vehicles are useful for delivering heavy items.

26. According to the article, which statement about Beijing in the 1980s is true?

   a. Bicycle parking was inconvenient.

   b. The air quality was acceptable.

   c. The air was unhealthy and unpleasant.

27. Which statement about Beijing is now true, according to the article?

    a. Road accidents are more common but not more serious.

    b. Road accidents are more serious but not more common.

    c. Road accidents are more common and more serious.

28. Which statement best describes the effect of motor vehicles on Beijing?

    a. Motor vehicles have made Beijing not only dirtier but also more dangerous.

    b. Motor vehicles have made Beijing neither dirtier nor more dangerous.

    c. Motor vehicles have made Beijing either dirtier or more dangerous.

29. According to the article, what has happened in Beijing since cars became popular there?

    a. Traffic has decreased.

    b. The air quality has become unacceptable.

    c. Transportation is now faster.

30. Which of the following best describes the condition of Beijing's streets today, according to the article?

    a. They have wide cycle lanes.

    b. They have plenty of convenient parking spots.

    c. They are overcrowded.

Choose one of the following topics to write about. Write a paragraph of at least four to five sentences.

- What kinds of behaviors in public places bother you most? Describe the behaviors and explain why they irritate you so much.

- Which urban problems do you think are the most serious? Explain. Use some of the words from the box.

discrimination	pollution	crime	unemployment
corruption	disease	crowding	lack of housing
poverty	inadequate public transportation		

31–33. ....

....

....

....

....

....

4

Name _____

Listening A

Part 1

🎧 **Listen to Part 1 of an announcer at an awards ceremony. Read the sentences. Then listen again and circle the letter of the answer that correctly completes each sentence.**

> **Example:** The speaker is announcing awards for people who _____.
>
> **a.** are talented and gifted   **(b.)** performed community service   **c.** won a contest

1. Mr. Williams got involved by _____.

   a. donating his heart at death   **b.** working without pay   **c.** planting flowers and trees

2. After attending camp with Mr. Williams, children became more _____.

   a. self-confident   **b.** self-conscious   **c.** self-critical

3. Mr. Williams could be described as a _____ because of his ability to work well with children.

   a. workaholic   **b.** people person   **c.** wise guy

4. The other camp counselors described Mr. Williams as a _____.

   a. brain   **b.** team player   **c.** workaholic

Part 2

🎧 **Listen to Part 2 of an announcer at an awards ceremony. Read the sentences. Then listen again and circle the letter of the answer that correctly completes each sentence.**

> **Example:** Mrs. Wells is _____.
>
> **a.** a librarian   **b.** a teacher   **(c.)** the president of a company

5. Mrs. Wells got involved by _____.

   a. raising money   **b.** beautifying the town   **c.** working without pay

6. Mrs. Wells could be described as _____.

   a. a spendthrift   **b.** generous   **c.** a tightwad

7. The speaker suggests that some people might find Mrs. Wells's contribution to be _____.

   a. egotistical   **b.** gifted   **c.** amazing

8. The speaker does not describe Mrs. Wells as being _____.

   a. passionate   **b.** energetic   **c.** a workaholic

Listening B

🎧 **Listen to the conversation. Read the questions. Then listen again and circle the letter of the correct answer.**

> **Example:** What did the father buy?
>
> **(a.)** a DVD player
>
> **b.** a VCR
>
> **c.** a new movie

9. Which statement about the father is true?

   a. He kept the VCR.

   b. When he bought the DVD player, he was worried that it might be a pain.

   c. He regrets not having kept the VCR.

10. Which statement about the son is true?

    a. He thinks VCRs are popular.

    b. He thinks VCRs are no longer popular.

    c. He thinks VCRs are hard to operate.

11. Which phrase does *not* describe the DVD player?

    a. old-fashioned

    b. hard to operate

    c. a pain

12. Which of the following is a problem with VCRs?

    a. It is difficult to find videotapes for newer movies.

    b. The manuals for them are too difficult to understand.

    c. They only play half a movie.

Circle the letter of the answer that correctly completes each sentence.

> **Example:** "I always leave big tips at restaurants. It's better to be generous than to be _____."
>
> **a.** gifted   **b.** energetic   **(c.)** cheap

13. "That dress would be perfect for the wedding. It's in good taste and is quite _____."

    a. shocking   **b.** elegant   **c.** gifted

14. "The violinist was talented but _____; she wore strange clothes and had her own way of doing things."

    a. eccentric   **b.** gifted   **c.** chic

15. "Don't be _____; the staff is starting to hate you because you're working them too hard."

    a. so egotistical   **b.** such a tyrant   **c.** such a cheapskate

16. "I love soul music, especially the love songs. They're so _____."

    a. tacky   **b.** difficult   **c.** passionate

17. "With its wild style and rainbow colors, her dress attracted a lot of attention. It was just too _____ for such a formal occasion."

    a. moody   **b.** flashy   **c.** stylish

18. "Matthew is buying all of us dinner? Great! I didn't realize he was _____."

    a. so frugal   **b.** so stingy   **c.** such a big spender

19. "Kyle doesn't make an effort to share his ideas or help other people in his group. He's just not _____."

    a. a team player   **b.** moody   **c.** a wise guy

20. "There's nothing wrong with being _____ if you're on a tight budget."

    a. thrifty   **b.** chic   **c.** difficult

21. "All heads turned toward the door when the tall, beautiful, _____ woman entered the room."

    a. tacky   **b.** striking   **c.** old-fashioned

**Form words by matching the correct prefixes with the adjectives below.
Complete each sentence with a word formed from the box.**

PREFIXES	ADJECTIVES
dis	~~mature~~
~~im~~	appropriate
un	imaginable
in	conscious
ir	honest
self-	rational

Example: "Candice is so _immature_ that no one would guess she is actually twenty-nine years old."

22. "For some reason, Steven seemed very worried about how he would look when we asked him if he would make a speech. I didn't know he was so _____."

23. "Blue jeans and sneakers are generally considered _____ for formal occasions."

24. "You'd have to see it to really understand; the beauty of the Sistine Chapel is

_____."

25. "That would give him the wrong impression; it would be false and _____."

26. "Fear of something that is actually harmless is _____."

Complete each sentence with the correct form of the verb in parentheses.

> **Example:** "She says she got a letter from me, but I don't remember _sending_ one."
> (send)

27. "Don't forget _____ to Martha to find out if she'll be coming
(write)
to our party this year."

28. "It's important to remember _____ off all cell phones and
(turn)
pagers when you're at a movie theater or concert hall."

29. "You really should stop _____ your friend Jim to visit.
(ask)
He's disrespectful to your parents and he's a troublemaker."

**Complete each sentence with either the simple past tense, the present
perfect, or the present perfect continuous form of the verb in parentheses.
Use the present perfect continuous if the action is unfinished or ongoing.**

> **Example:** " _Have you traveled_ to Europe before? Or is this your first time?"
> (travel)

30. "That last song sounded much better than before. It's obvious that
you _____."
(practice)

31. "Does anyone know how long they _____ together?"
(perform)

32. "She _____ Pavarotti perform several times when she lived in New York."
(see)

Circle the letter of the answer that correctly completes each sentence.

> **Example:** We have _____ problems: where to go and how to get there.
>
>   **a.** few   **b.** many   (c.) two

33. _____ company has its own unique challenges and problems.

    a. Every   **b.** Most   **c.** All

34. Our staff is smaller now, and _____ employees means _____ days off for everyone.

    a. less, less   **b.** fewer, fewer   **c.** fewer, less

35. _____ employees want to change the vacation schedule.

    a. Every   **b.** Some   **c.** Any

Read each sentence. Write a sentence expressing your opinion about it. Use a possessive with a gerund and one of the verbs in the box.

appreciate	like	mind	object

> **Example:** A woman who works with you smokes in the office.
>   *I don't like her smoking in the office.*

36. Your colleague listens to music all the time while he is working.

    _____

37. You started a new job where everyone dresses in casual attire on Fridays.

    _____

38. Your colleague often talks on the phone to his friends while he is at work.

    _____

Complete each sentence in your own way. Write about your plans or goals for the future.

> **Example:** By the time _I'm 21_, I hope _to have graduated from college_.

39. When I _____, I'll _____.

40. By this time next year, I plan _____.

41. Once _____, I'll _____.

Read the short biography. Then read it again and check <u>true</u> or <u>false</u>.

Howard Hughes

ENGINEER, PILOT, MOVIE PRODUCER
1905 — 1976

*Eccentric billionaire, Howard Hughes was
a major figure of the 20th century.*

Howard Hughes was born in 1905, to a wealthy family in the Texas oil industry. By the age of eleven, Hughes had demonstrated genius in math and mechanical engineering—once building a motorcycle from parts taken from a steam engine. At fourteen, he took his first flying lesson. These early experiments were the beginning of his lifelong passions for aviation and engineering. As a teenager, Hughes declared that his goals in life were to be the world's best golfer, its greatest pilot, and its most famous movie producer. Amazingly, during his lifetime he achieved two of these ambitions.

On his father's death in 1924, the nineteen-year-old Hughes inherited Hughes Tool Company, valued at a million dollars. Hughes used his wealth to become a Hollywood film producer. His films included *Hell's Angels,* a fighter pilot epic that Hughes spent four years and a record $3.8 million to make. A demanding director, Hughes once stopped production for months to wait for a specific type of cloud to appear in the sky. Once, when his pilots refused to attempt a particularly dangerous stunt, Hughes flew it himself—getting the shot but crashing the plane. When the film was nearly complete, Hughes decided that silent movies were outdated and reshot the film with sound. A box office success, *Hell's Angels* cemented Hughes' reputation for thinking big and never hesitating to go in new directions.

In 1932, Hughes founded Hughes Aircraft. As a pilot and self-taught engineer, he set many world speed records and made significant advances in aviation technology. His H-1 Racer was the fastest plane in the world and his H-4 Hercules flying boat was the largest plane ever built.

However, as Hughes aged, he started to become more and more eccentric. Before eating peas, for example, he would sort them by size on his plate. Fearful of germs, he avoided shaking hands with people. By the 1950s, his health had deteriorated and he disappeared, living in hotel rooms with blacked-out windows. Rumors circulated about his strange lifestyle—that he wore tissue boxes as shoes and that he used paper towels to cover any object before he touched it. When Hughes died in 1976, he was so changed that fingerprints had to be used to identify his body.

Sources: http://en.wikipedia.org; www.socalhistory.org

		true	false
Example:	The article describes a creative personality.	☑	☐

		true	false
42.	Howard Hughes was gifted in math and engineering.	☐	☐
43.	Hughes was passionate about one thing: the oil industry.	☐	☐
44.	As a teenager, Hughes didn't have the self-confidence to become successful.	☐	☐
45.	As a movie producer, Hughes was famous for being a big spender.	☐	☐
46.	Pilots on the set of the film *Hell's Angels* described Hughes as a sweetheart.	☐	☐
47.	As a director, Hughes was not very energetic and he tried to not get too involved in the films he made.	☐	☐
48.	Hughes was an old-fashioned director who preferred silent movies to movies with sound.	☐	☐
49.	Hughes was never self-critical; once he started something, he would never change direction, even if he thought he had made a mistake.	☐	☐
50.	Hughes was an imaginative man who was not afraid to try new things.	☐	☐
51.	Hughes was a brain who taught himself how to design airplanes.	☐	☐
52.	Later in life, Hughes became known for his increasingly eccentric behavior.	☐	☐
53.	A real people person, Hughes had a smile and a handshake for everyone he met.	☐	☐
54.	Hughes remained energetic, piloting airplanes and directing films until his death in 1976.	☐	☐

Choose two of the following topics to write about. Write a paragraph of at least four to five sentences for each topic.

- Describe a major personality change that you have seen in someone you know. What was that person like before? What is he or she like now? What caused this change?

- Describe your favorite musician or band.

- Imagine that you will be starting your own business. What steps will you take? What plans will you make and how will you carry them out? How successful do you think you will be?

- Describe the difference between the fashions of your childhood and those of today. What has changed and how?

- Identify a problem in your town or city. What do you think should be done to solve it? Who should be responsible for fixing it?

55–57. ....

....

....

....

....

58–60. ....

....

....

....

....

Name _____

Choose one of the following topics. On a separate sheet of paper, write an essay of at least three paragraphs. You will have 5 minutes to choose a topic and 30 minutes to write your essay.

Topic One

What are some of your goals in life? What are some ways in which you would like to improve yourself? The following are some possible ideas:

- Personal goals (getting involved with your community, finding balance in your life)
- Financial goals (sticking to a budget, making charitable contributions)
- Professional goals (learning to work as a team player, being passionate about your work)

Topic Two

What are some things that people do that really get on your nerves? The following are some possible ideas:

- At work (dress inappropriately, have difficult or egotistical personalities, gossip)
- In public (litter, talk on cell phones, dress offensively)
- At home (forget to do things around the house, become easily annoyed, have pessimistic viewpoints)

Name _____

Choose one of the following topics. Give a short talk of about 3 minutes to either your teacher or the whole class. You will have 5 minutes to prepare.

- Describe a life-changing experience. What happened? How did you react? Do you think you reacted the way you did because of your personality? Explain. Did the experience change your self-image or affect your self-esteem in any way? If so, how?

- Describe someone you know well. What is your relationship to him or her? How would you describe his or her personality? Do you consider this person to be generous, stingy, or somewhere in between? Explain. Does he or she ever do anything that gets on your nerves? Explain.

- What type of personality do you have? How does your taste in music and fashion reflect your personality? Do you think your personality affects your spending habits in any way? Explain.

Name _____

🎧 **Listen to the conversation. Read the sentences. Then listen again and check true or false.**

		true	false
Example:	The man and woman are discussing their favorite pets.	☑	☐
1.	The man thought that dogs were difficult to take care of.	☐	☐
2.	The woman thinks that it might be all right to leave dogs home alone for a long time.	☐	☐
3.	The woman thinks that pit bulls are never aggressive.	☐	☐
4.	The woman raised her pit bull for fighting.	☐	☐
5.	The woman describes her pit bull as being good-natured with other pets.	☐	☐
6.	The man describes his pet iguana as friendly and loving.	☐	☐

Complete the paragraph with words from the box.

aggressive	~~affectionate~~	destructive	adorable	filthy	costly

People love their pets, but they shouldn't expect everyone else to do the same.

Sometimes a pet that is very friendly and ___*affectionate*___ with its owner can be

               Example

_____ or even violent with strangers. Pets can also damage property such

       7.

as furniture. You may think your pet is cute and _____ and that everyone

                                 8.

should love it no matter what it does. But if your pet is unclean, or _____, or

                                          9.

if it is _____ to property, then it is a problem for everyone. Just because you

        10.

might not mind paying a lot to maintain a _____ animal doesn't mean others

                                 11.

will be understanding if they have to pay to replace things damaged by your pet.

Circle the letter of the answer that correctly completes each sentence.

Example:	"Don't tell Martha that you hate her cat. That would be _____."
	a. gullible **(b.)** mean **c.** wise

12. "Come away from that mirror and stop being so _____."

    a. gullible   **b.** mean   **c.** vain

13. "I don't think he was telling us the truth about why he was late. He didn't sound _____."

    a. sincere   **b.** selfish   **c.** gullible

14. "You should try talking to your grandmother about your problem. She's very _____."

    a. vain   **b.** wise   **c.** gullible

15. "I've heard that pigs are even more _____ than dogs. They can learn all kinds of really difficult tricks."

    a. clever   **b.** selfish   **c.** gullible

Complete each sentence, using the words in parentheses.

Example: "Sharks are fascinating creatures, but they _can't be kept_ as pets."
                                                        (can / not / keep)

16. "I think it's wrong to test beauty products on animals; only lifesaving medicines _____ on them."
                    (should / test)

17. "Dogs are used to help people with disabilities, but I read an article that said cats _____ just as easily."
                    (could / use)

18. "If people knew what happens to abandoned pets, animals _____
                                            (might / not / give)
as gifts so often."

19. "The killing of African elephants _____, or they will become extinct
                                (have / stop)
very soon."

20. "In the computer age, why do animals _____ for research?"
                                (have / use)

Read each statement. Write a sentence expressing your opinion about each statement. Use the passive voice with modals.

Example: Animals are used for medical research.

    Animals shouldn't be used for medical research because it's cruel.

21. Animals are killed for their hides and fur.

_____

22. Animals are trained to help people with disabilities.

_____

23. Animals are kept in zoos.

_____

Read the website. Then read it again and circle the letter of the answer that correctly completes each sentence.

PetMatch.com

Amazon Parrots

Amazon parrots are bright, colorful birds native to South and Central America. These popular pets are highly intelligent and very talkative. They love to mimic their owners' voices and other sounds in their environment. They also enjoy being handled and are very loving—often becoming very attached to their owners. Amazons love to climb, play with toys, and even show off cute tricks like tossing a ring or using roller skates.

Amazons can be costly, both to purchase and to care for. With an average length of 10–18 inches (25–45 cm), they are large birds and each requires a cage 39–59 inches (100–150 cm) high, with a floor space of at least 23 x 39 inches (60 x 100 cm). To ensure proper nutrition, an Amazon's diet should include a mix of parrot food pellets and seeds as well as fresh fruits and vegetables. Food and water dishes must be cleaned daily and cages weekly. Weekly baths are also necessary to keep feathers in good shape.

Amazons are very social birds. They need a lot of attention and will become lonely and unhappy if left alone for long periods. They are often friendly with older children who know how to interact properly with them but need to be watched carefully around younger children. Although Amazons can develop close friendships with some other pets, they can be a danger to smaller animals such as hamsters, mice, or small birds. Amazons have powerful beaks and enjoy chewing—if allowed outside of their cages, care should be taken to protect furniture and other belongings from damage. While Amazons are generally calm, they can be noisy in the early morning and at sunset.

Home • Petfinder • Animal Health • Links

Example: According to the website, a positive trait of Amazon parrots is that they are _____.

    a. destructive   **b.** low maintenance   **c.** devoted

24. According to the website, a negative trait of Amazon parrots is that they are _____.

    a. costly   **b.** adorable   **c.** low maintenance

25. Amazon parrots can be aggressive; for example, they are _____.

    a. friendly with other pets   **b.** quite noisy   **c.** a danger to smaller animals

26. People find Amazon parrots adorable because they _____.

    a. learn tricks   **b.** make a mess   **c.** damage furniture

27. Amazon parrots are loyal; for example, they often _____.

    a. have colorful feathers   **b.** can talk and learn tricks   **c.** become very attached to their owners

28. Amazon parrots are high maintenance; for example, they _____.

    a. need a lot of attention   **b.** are expensive to buy   **c.** love to climb and play with toys

29. An Amazon parrot would be a good pet for a person who _____.

    a. owns expensive wood furniture   **b.** has a three-year-old child   **c.** spends a lot of time at home

30. A person who _____ should not consider getting an Amazon parrot.

    a. spends a lot of time at home   **b.** is noisy   **c.** wants an inexpensive pet

Choose one of the following topics to write about. Write a paragraph of at least four to five sentences.

- How do you feel about using animals for medical research?
- Describe your favorite pet.

31–33. _____

_____

_____

_____

_____

Name _____

🎧 **Listen to each conversation. Read the questions. Then listen again and circle the letter of the correct answer.**

> **Example:** They are _____.
>   **a.** haggling
>   **(b.)** comparison shopping
>   **c.** window-shopping

Conversation A

1. The woman is _____.

    a. browsing

    b. window-shopping

    c. shopping around

2. The woman _____.

    a. is being asked to help

    b. is looking to be helped

    c. does not want to be helped

Conversation B

3. The two people are _____.

    a. window-shopping

    b. browsing

    c. haggling

4. The customer _____.

    a. expected to be told the truth

    b. did not expect to be told the truth

    c. resents being lied to

Conversation C

5. The couple is _____.

    a. comparison shopping

    b. window-shopping

    c. shopping around

6. The woman _____.

    a. likes being offered a bargain

    b. resents being reminded that they were not planning to buy anything

    c. is annoyed about being told they were trying to spend less

Complete each sentence with a word or phrase from the box.

browse	haggle
bargain-hunt	shop around
window-shop	~~comparison shop~~

Example: "I'm not going to buy the first car I see—I prefer to *comparison shop* ."

7. "Whenever I go into a store, I buy something I can't afford. Let's not go into any stores today; let's just _____ as we walk through town."

8. "The best thing about shopping at the street market is that you don't have to pay the first price you get from sellers. You can _____ with them to get a better price."

9. "I need to get some new clothes for work, but I don't have a lot of money. I'm going to seriously _____ . I won't stop until I know I've found the lowest prices in town."

10. "That looks like a nice watch, but that doesn't mean it's good quality. I think you should _____ some more and do some research before you buy one."

11. "I go into bookstores all the time, but I hardly ever buy anything; I just _____ ."

Complete each conversation with an expression from the box. Make changes as necessary.

~~drive me crazy~~	get on my nerves
blow me away	choke me up
crack me up	

Example: **A:** My son is such a troublemaker!

        B: Oh, yeah? What's he up to now?

        A: Well, this morning he was disrespectful to his grandma. He makes me so angry.

        B: Well, if it makes you feel better, my daughter *drives me crazy* , too. She never listens to anything I say.

12. **A:** This Al Green CD is amazing. I haven't heard music this great in a long time.

      B: I know. Every time I listen to the song "Tired of Being Alone," his voice just

      _____ .

13. **A:** What did you think of *Napoleon Dynamite*?

      B: I loved it. When Napoleon did his goofy dance at the end of the movie, I couldn't stop laughing!

      A: Yeah, that _____ , too.

14. **A:** How was your sister's wedding?

    B: Oh, it was really lovely. She looked so beautiful.

    A: Did you cry?

    B: Of course I did. You know me, weddings always _____.

15. **A:** Would you mind changing the station?

    B: Why? I thought you liked country music.

    A: I do, but I hate this DJ. His voice is so annoying. And he's always talking.

    B: Yeah, I know what you mean. It always _____ when radio DJs talk too much.

Complete each sentence with the correct form of the verb in parentheses.

Example: "I resent *being forced* to listen to loud rock music while I'm browsing
                       (force)
in record shops."

16. "I want _____ for what I've done, not for what I had."
              (remember)

17. "People always enjoy _____ while they're having dinner."
                         (entertain)

18. "I didn't expect _____ the truth, but the salesman was very honest with me."
                     (tell)

19. "Claire really appreciates _____ like a movie star when she goes shopping."
                               (treat)

20. "The band was disappointed _____ to perform at the festival this year."
                               (not / ask)

Complete each sentence in your own way. Use a passive gerund or infinitive.

Example: You're lucky *to be given such a great opportunity* .

21. I don't expect _____.

22. They resent _____.

23. We enjoy _____.

Read the article. Then read it again and circle the word or phrase that correctly completes each sentence.

Back   Forward   Stop   Refresh   Home   Print   Mail   Search

Address: @ http://www.shopsmart.com   〉 go

Favorites
History
Search

Tips for Savvy Online Shopping

Bargain-hunt:

- Get on mailing lists. Sign up with your favorite stores to receive news about sales and special offers by e-mail.

- Compare prices. Comparison websites such as Froogle.com and Bizrate.com allow you to quickly find the cheapest prices across the Web on any product you're looking for.

- Search for deals. Type the name of the store you want to buy from along with the words "coupon code" into a search engine such as Google.com. Many large stores regularly offer discounts such as free shipping.

Do your homework:

- Read product reviews from experts and other customers on sites such as ConsumerReports.org or Epinions.com before making a purchase.

Always be careful about online security and safety:

- Shop only at secure sites. Make sure a website is safe by looking for signs such as "https" in a website's address bar, or icons such as an unbroken key ⌇ or a padlock 🔒 at the bottom of a screen.

- Don't give your personal or credit card information to a seller who asks for it by e-mail.

- Check your credit card statements carefully and call your credit card company immediately if you notice any charges that you don't recognize.

Cut back on shipping costs:

- Try to purchase from sellers as close to you as possible. International shipping fees in particular can be quite high.

- Order early so that you don't have to pay extra for express delivery.

- Ship items together. Buying several purchases at the same time, at a single store, can be much cheaper than buying the same items at several different stores.

- Check return policies and be aware that you may have to pay shipping charges to return items you don't want to keep.

Home • Login • My Account • Help • Links

4

Example: You can save time (shopping around)/ promoting by using websites such as <u>Froogle.com</u>.

24. According to the article, it is easy to **haggle / comparison shop** on the Web.

25. You should not buy something online without being **informed / persuaded**.

26. A seller who asks for your credit card information by e-mail might be trying to **tell you about a good deal / steal from you**.

27. To save on shipping costs, you should try to buy **one thing / several things** at a time.

28. International shipping costs can be **a bit steep / a good deal**.

29. The article **implies / proves** that people can save money by shopping online.

30. The article gives advice on how to **splurge / find great offers** while shopping online.

Choose one of the following topics to write about. Write a paragraph of at least four to five sentences.

- Are you or is anyone you know a compulsive shopper? Describe this behavior. Use some of the words from the box.

- Describe an impulse buy that you regret making. Use some of the words from the box.

indulge yourself	go overboard
resist the temptation	get the urge
overspending	splurge on

31–33. _____

_____

_____

_____

_____

Name _____

🎧 **Listen to the conversation. Read the sentences. Then listen again and circle the word or phrase that correctly completes each sentence.**

> **Example:** Mark saw **Ellen /** (**Janet**) at the mall.

1. **Mark / Ellen** is sure that Janet will shape up.
2. Janet and Ellen's parents treated their daughters **the same / differently**.
3. Janet and Ellen's parents are more **strict / lenient** with Janet than they were with Ellen.
4. Ellen was a **rebellious / well-behaved** teenager.
5. Janet is more **disrespectful / overprotective** of her parents' rules than Ellen was.
6. Ellen's parents were **overprotective / lenient** with her because they worried about her safety.
7. Mark thinks Janet is **too lenient / a little spoiled**.

Write the noun form of each verb or adjective on the line.

> **Example:** different → _difference_

8. happy → _____
9. expect → _____
10. responsible → _____
11. develop → _____
12. important → _____

Combine each pair of sentences into one new sentence. Use repeated comparatives.

> **Example:** The birthrate is low now. It was not as low before.
>
> _The birthrate is getting lower and lower._

13. Life expectancy is high now. It was not as high before.

   _____

14. Divorce is common now. It was not as common before.

   _____

15. People are working longer hours now. They did not work such long hours before.

   _____

16. Health care is good now. It was not as good before.

   _____

Combine each pair of sentences into one new sentence. Use double comparatives.

> <u>Example:</u>   **Cause:** Couples are waiting longer to have children.
>
>   **Effect:** Couples are having fewer children.
>
>   _The longer couples wait to have children, the fewer they have._

17. **Cause:** People are living longer.

   Effect: People are requiring more care.

   _____

18. **Cause:** Health care is getting better.

   Effect: Life expectancy is getting higher.

   _____

19. **Cause:** Life expectancy is getting higher.

   Effect: The elderly population is getting larger.

   _____

20. **Cause:** People work hard.

   Effect: They are successful.

   _____

Complete the first sentence by defining the group of people. Complete the second sentence with an example of typical behavior for the group.

> <u>Example:</u> Rebellious teenagers _don't obey the rules_ .
>
>   They _stay out late without permission_ .

21. Spoiled teenagers _____ .

   They _____ .

22. Overprotective parents _____ .

   They _____ .

23. Lenient parents _____ .

   They _____ .

Read the newspaper article. Then read it again and circle the letter of the correct answer.

Britain faces the challenge of a declining population

Statistics show British women are having children later in life.

Government statistics show that family patterns in Great Britain are changing. The government has been tracking birth records to determine the average age at which women have children. If a woman has one child when she is 21 and a second when she is 23, her average age for having children is 22. The average for all British women born in 1940 was 26. For women born in the mid-1970s, it is projected to be just over 29. It is rising slowly and will eventually be over 30 if the present trend continues.

Not only are British women having children later and later in life, they are having fewer and fewer of them. British women born in 1934 had an average of 2.46 children. For women born in 1955, that number dropped to 2.03. No one is sure exactly why this happened, but unless there is a sudden change in the pattern, the number will drop to 1.74 for the generation of women born in the 1980s.

Additionally, more and more women are choosing not to have children at all. Only 9% of British women born in 1945 and 1946 chose to remain childless. For the generation of women who are now reaching the end of their childbearing years, that number has increased to almost 20%. The more these trends continue, the smaller the population will get.

Such changes in birthrate and family patterns are creating many challenges for the government. A declining population is likely to cause problems for the social welfare system, for example. As the population declines, there will be fewer taxpayers to support the sick, disabled, and retired.

These issues promise to have no ready answers or easy solutions. For instance, recent government initiatives to discourage teenagers from having children they cannot afford to raise without public financial assistance have been successful. However, this will also contribute to the decline in population growth. From another perspective, environmentalists see the population decline as a positive development; there will be fewer users of limited natural resources. As one can see, public policy on population growth is extremely complex.

Source: www.statistics.gov.uk

Example: According to the first paragraph, _____.

   a. the British government wants women to have children younger

   b. the British government keeps information about childbirth

   c. present trends in childbirth will continue in Britain

24. According to the second paragraph, _____.

   a. British women are having children earlier and earlier

   b. there is no obvious explanation for the change in childbearing patterns in Britain

   c. there was no difference between the birthrate in 1934 and the birthrate in 1955 in Britain

25. The number of childless women in Britain is _____.

   a. staying the same

   b. going down

   c. going up

26. The number of _____ is decreasing.

   a. taxpayers

   b. older people

   c. people who need social services

27. One positive aspect of a declining population is that it _____.

   a. is good for the environment

   b. is bad for the environment

   c. creates limited natural resources

28. According to the last paragraph, _____.

   a. more unmarried teenagers are having babies

   b. the British government has discouraged unmarried teenagers from having babies

   c. the reduction in unmarried teen parenthood has created an easy solution

29. According to the article, _____.

   a. the rate of population growth in Britain is getting higher and higher

   b. British women are having more and more children, and having them earlier and earlier

   c. British women are having fewer and fewer children, and having them later and later

30. The trend in Britain is toward _____ motherhood.

   a. earlier

   b. later

   c. teenage

Choose one of the following topics to write about. Write a paragraph of at least four to five sentences.

- What trends do you see happening in families? Do you think these trends are good or bad?

- How does your generation differ from the one that comes before or after it?

31–33. _____

_____

_____

_____

_____

_____

Name _____

🎧 **Listen to the conversation. Read the questions. The listen again and circle the letter of the correct answer.**

> **Example:** What is "Man-made Mysteries"?
> **ⓐ** It's a television program.
> **b.** It's a radio program.
> **c.** It's a science textbook.

1. How does the woman feel about the stone balls of Costa Rica?

   a. It's possible that she's interested in them.

   b. She probably isn't interested in them.

   c. Clearly, she's interested in them.

2. What does the man first think about the stone balls?

   a. He thinks it's possible they occurred naturally.

   b. He thinks there's no question they were man-made.

   c. He thinks it's obvious they were man-made.

3. What did the show say about the stone balls?

   a. They could have occurred naturally.

   b. It's not possible to know how they were formed.

   c. They had to have been man-made.

4. Which of the following do the man and woman speculate about?

   a. They discuss what the stone balls could have possibly been used for.

   b. They discuss who the sculptor who made the stone balls could have been.

   c. They discuss how long it might have taken to make the stone balls.

5. Does the woman think that the stone balls could have fallen from space?

   a. She thinks it's likely they did.

   b. She thinks the idea is very questionable.

   c. She thinks it seems possible that they may have.

6. What do the man and woman disagree about?

   a. They disagree about the possible use of the stone balls.

   b. They disagree about the date the stone balls were discovered.

   c. They disagree about the size of the stone balls.

Read each statement. Check <u>certain</u> or <u>not certain</u>.

		certain	not certain
Example:	"The conservative candidate will most likely win the election this year."	☐	☑
7.	"I left my purse on the train. I'll call the lost-and-found; maybe someone turned it in."	☐	☐
8.	"It's possible that it might rain tomorrow."	☐	☐
9.	"Look at all this traffic! There's no question we're going to miss our flight. We'll have to catch the later one."	☐	☐

Read each statement. Then write sentences, using expressions of certainty to speculate about what happened.

Example: "A loud noise woke me last night, but I have no idea what it was."

Maybe your cat knocked something over.

10. "I came to class at the right time, but the classroom was empty."

_____

11. "The door to Jack's apartment was open and the lights were on, but no one was home."

_____

12. "I can't find my wallet or my keys. They were in my pocket when I left the house this morning."

_____

Complete each sentence with a word from the box. You will not use all of the words.

~~questionable~~	debatable
believable	probable
unsolvable	provable

Example: Since the study was flawed, its results are very *questionable* _____.

13. With no witnesses or proof, the mystery is _____.

14. The question of whether or not solar power is the answer to the energy crisis is

_____. Experts offer many other solutions as well.

15. There are several theories about the mystery of the Bermuda Triangle, but with so

little evidence, none are _____.

Read the e-mail from Sally to Monica. Then complete the e-mail from Monica to Kathleen, using the correct modals.

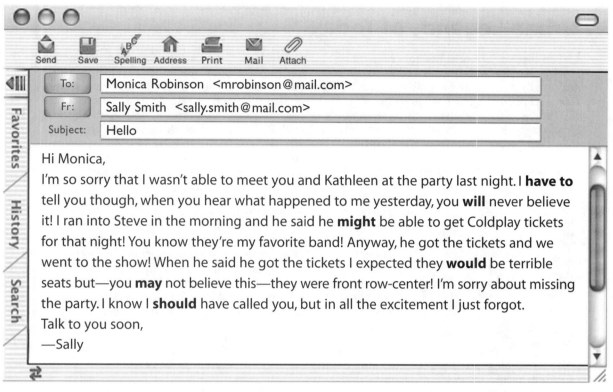

To: Monica Robinson <mrobinson@mail.com>
Fr: Sally Smith <sally.smith@mail.com>
Subject: Hello

Hi Monica,

I'm so sorry that I wasn't able to meet you and Kathleen at the party last night. I **have to** tell you though, when you hear what happened to me yesterday, you **will** never believe it! I ran into Steve in the morning and he said he **might** be able to get Coldplay tickets for that night! You know they're my favorite band! Anyway, he got the tickets and we went to the show! When he said he got the tickets I expected they **would** be terrible seats but—you **may** not believe this—they were front row-center! I'm sorry about missing the party. I know I **should** have called you, but in all the excitement I just forgot.
Talk to you soon,
—Sally

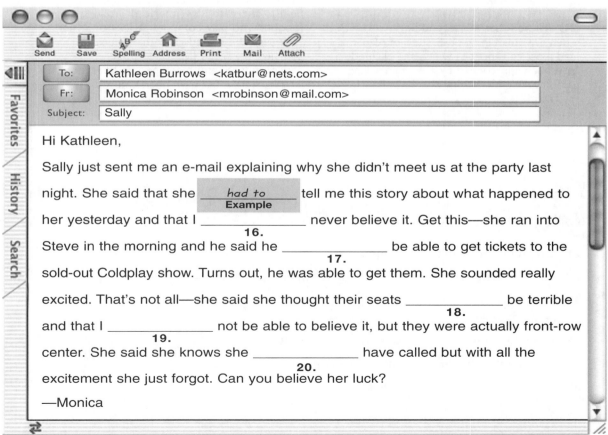

To: Kathleen Burrows <katbur@nets.com>
Fr: Monica Robinson <mrobinson@mail.com>
Subject: Sally

Hi Kathleen,

Sally just sent me an e-mail explaining why she didn't meet us at the party last night. She said that she ___had to___ tell me this story about what happened to
                                Example
her yesterday and that I _____ never believe it. Get this—she ran into
                              16.
Steve in the morning and he said he _____ be able to get tickets to the
                                      17.
sold-out Coldplay show. Turns out, he was able to get them. She sounded really

excited. That's not all—she said she thought their seats _____ be terrible
                                                          18.
and that I _____ not be able to believe it, but they were actually front-row
            19.
center. She said she knows she _____ have called but with all the
                                20.
excitement she just forgot. Can you believe her luck?

—Monica

Read the magazine article. Then read it again and check <u>true</u> or <u>false</u>.

Urban Legends of Today

Urban legends are questionable or strange stories that are widely accepted as true. They are usually somewhat believable because they relate to normal day-to-day activities, but they are also usually surprising or even scary. Urban legends now spread faster and wider than ever before because of the Internet.

One well-known, but unproved, urban legend is about so-called "perfume bandits." According to the legend, criminals approach people and pretend to be selling perfume. When victims come close to see or smell the perfume, the bandits spray something in their faces, knocking them out for a period of time during which the bandits rob them.

It is believed that this legend began in 1999 when a woman in the U.S. state of Alabama, filed a police report in which she claimed to have been approached by a woman selling perfume. The next thing she said she remembered was having something sprayed in her face and then later waking up in a parking lot without her purse. However, since perfume does not leave physical evidence, the police were unable to confirm the facts or catch the robbers. The police finally closed the case and stamped the file "unsolvable." However, similar stories have been reported by others, and a large number of people still believe that the perfume bandits actually exist.

Another urban legend is that of the "haiku error messages." According to this legend, programmers working for a software company in Japan replaced standard computer error messages with haikus—traditional 3-line, Japanese poems. For example, when a document could not be found the following "haiku" would appear on the screen:

> Having been erased,
> The document you're seeking
> Must now be retyped.

These haiku error messages turned out to be a joke created by American "hackers" (people who play computer tricks on others). However, the legend grew that there actually *were* some Japanese "poet-programmers" and many people believed it. The hackers must have been amused.

	true	false
Example: Urban legends are usually somewhat believable.	☑	☐
21. Urban legends can be frightening.	☐	☐
22. Today, urban legends spread less quickly than they did in the past.	☐	☐
23. The police were unable to prove whether or not the perfume bandits actually existed.	☐	☐
24. It is now known the legend of the perfume bandits was a hoax.	☐	☐
25. The people who wrote the haikus were Japanese.	☐	☐
26. The hackers were probably pleased with their joke.	☐	☐

Circle the letter of the answer that correctly completes each sentence.

Example: "The Incas didn't have any sophisticated machines or use any work animals. Their temples _____ been built solely through manual labor."
a. must not have   (**b.**) must have   **c.** may have

27. "My keys aren't on the table where I always leave them. They _____ been taken by my husband."

    a. may have   **b.** had   **c.** had not

28. "Dinosaurs didn't necessarily die off gradually from climate change; they _____ been killed off quickly by some sudden event."

    a. could have   **b.** couldn't have   **c.** had

29. "I don't believe in any of the other theories. There is no doubt: Stonehenge _____ been built by the ancient Britons."

    a. might have   **b.** might not have   **c.** had to have

30. "Some of the visitors brought only long pants and sweaters; they _____ been told that it's so hot and humid here."

    a. must have   **b.** must not have   **c.** could have

Choose one of the mysteries from the box or think of something mysterious that has happened in your own life. Write a paragraph of at least four to five sentences.

The Loch Ness Monster	Bigfoot
The Bermuda Triangle	Atlantis
The Stone Balls of Costa Rica	The Nazca Lines
The Explosion in Tunguska	Stonehenge

31–33. _____

_____

_____

_____

_____

Name _____

🎧 **Listen to the conversation. Read the sentences. Then listen again and circle the letter of the answer that correctly completes each sentence.**

> **Example:** Gail and Jeff are discussing their _____ .
>
>   **a.** families   **(b.)** hobbies   **c.** jobs

1. Gail's hobby right now is _____ .

   a. restoring antiques   **b.** yoga   **c.** karate

2. Gail says that one of the reasons she took up her new hobby is that she was getting _____ .

   a. out of shape   **b.** a good job   **c.** too busy

3. Jeff is surprised that Gail _____ .

   a. has enough time for karate   **b.** likes selling furniture   **c.** has a new job

4. Gail wanted a hobby that had more _____ benefits.

   a. intellectual   **b.** physical   **c.** financial

5. Gail _____ karate.

   a. is tired of   **b.** can't get enough of   **c.** wouldn't dare try

6. Jeff does _____ .

   a. karate   **b.** furniture restoring   **c.** yoga

Match the words in the columns below to form collocations for leisure activities.

Example: _____e_____ antiques	**a.** play
7. _____ a hobby	**b.** do
8. _____ iguanas	**c.** have
9. _____ chess	**d.** collect
10. _____ stamps	~~e.~~ restore
11. _____ yoga	**f.** raise

Complete each sentence by writing the noun modifiers in parentheses in the correct order.

> **Example:** This is _Jack's first real_____ vacation in five years.
>   **(first / Jack's / real)**

12. Angelina brought a _____ scarf back from her trip.
              (silk / French / beautiful)

13. We met a _____ man on the bus.
(nice / Chinese / young)

14. The city library has _____ books.
(interesting / some / history)

15. The class gave Marie a _____ bowl as a going-away present.
(huge / round / glass)

16. Jed has _____ comic books in his collection.
(old / one thousand / rare)

Complete each sentence with a word from the box. You will not use all of the words.

| creatively | emotionally | financially | intellectually |
| physically | socially | spiritually | |

Example: My painting teacher wanted us to copy the Old Masters. It was interesting but not
creatively stimulating.

17. Extreme sports are thrilling but can be _____ dangerous.

18. Gambling can be fun, but be careful—it can set you back _____.

19. Markus doesn't tend to make many new friends; he isn't very skilled _____.

20. Relationships are usually _____ satisfying when people can spend a lot of time together and feel that they can rely on each other.

21. I enjoy playing chess because I find it _____ stimulating; few games require so much concentration and careful thought.

Write a sentence about each activity below. Use expressions of fear or fearlessness to describe how you feel about each activity.

Example: waterfall jumping
You wouldn't catch me waterfall jumping.

22. surfing

23. white-water rafting

24. hang gliding

Read the magazine article. Then read it again and check <u>true</u> or <u>false</u>.

Are the "Leisure" Activities of Today's Teens Unhealthy and Overstimulating?

by Dave Williams

Teenagers today have an ever-increasing number of ways to entertain themselves. With the advent of cell phones, cable TV, the Internet, and high-tech video games, etc., teens have countless means of amusement at their fingertips. Teens no longer have merely one or two hobbies that they divide their time between. Gone are the days when teens spent their free time simply playing ping-pong or collecting coins. Now teens' typical leisure-time activities involve a myriad of technical devices that are often used simultaneously. For a glimpse of today's frenetic teen life, look at an instant message conversation between two sixteen-year-olds:

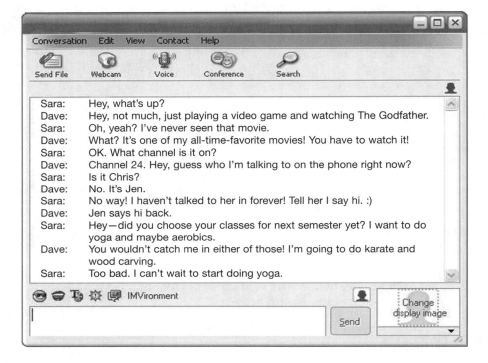

Some researchers think that the conversation above represents an all-too-common scenario for teens today. They are concerned that the habit of doing so many things at the same time may be detrimental intellectually. Some wonder if this is one reason students are having an increasingly difficult time paying attention and focusing on one thing at a time in school. Additionally, many are concerned that spending so much time doing things that are not physically active may be contributing to the increase in obesity among teens. Others simply say that the way that teens spend their leisure time today may actually be overstimulating and not relaxing.

	true	false
Example: Dave would like to do yoga and wood carving.	☐	☑
25. Technology has changed the way teens spend their free time.	☐	☐
26. Dave is having an instant message conversation, watching a movie, playing a video game, and talking on the phone all at once.	☐	☐
27. Sara is only involved in one activity: instant messaging.	☐	☐
28. Sara is not afraid to do yoga.	☐	☐
29. Teens today often prefer to do only one thing at a time, rather than several things at once.	☐	☐
30. Most leisure-time activities teens engage in today are physically challenging.	☐	☐

Choose one of the following topics to write about. Write a paragraph of at least four to five sentences.

• What is your favorite leisure activity and what benefits do you get from it?

• Do you enjoy taking risks? Explain why or why not and provide examples.

31–33. ....

....

....

....

....

....

Name _____

Listening A

🎧 **Listen to the advertisement. Read the sentences. Then listen again and circle the letter of the answer that correctly completes each sentence.**

> **Example:** This advertisement is for _____.
>
> **ⓐ** a karate school
>
> **b.** a class for parents
>
> **c.** a home-study course

1. The announcer in the advertisement is speaking to _____.

   a. children who want to have a hobby

   b. parents who want to have a hobby

   c. parents who want their children to shape up

2. The advertisement describes the problem of _____.

   a. parents who expect their kids to obey too many rules

   b. children who refuse to follow rules

   c. parents who let their kids do anything they want

3. The advertisement implies that karate helps children become less _____.

   a. obedient

   b. respectful

   c. dependent

4. The advertisement describes how today, more and more _____.

   a. parents are being too lenient

   b. kids are being spoiled

   c. kids are rude to adults and refuse to follow their rules

5. The advertisement recommends that parents of children who act up should _____.

   a. enroll their kids in the karate class

   b. be less strict

   c. not be so overprotective

6. The advertisement states that in the karate class, kids will be able to work out their _____.

    a. friendly and loving tendencies

    b. violent feelings

    c. easygoing natures

7. The advertisement promises growth that is _____.

    a. physical but not emotional or spiritual

    b. emotional and spiritual but not physical

    c. physical, emotional, and spiritual

Listening B

🎧 **Listen to the conversation. Read the questions. Then listen again and circle the letter of the correct answer.**

Example: The man and woman are talking about _____.
    ⓐ shopping   **b.** the economy   **c.** scary stories

8. The woman's problem is that she _____.

    a. cannot find any deals   **b.** spends too much money   **c.** is worried about the economy

9. The woman _____ sticking to a budget.

    a. is not capable of   **b.** succeeded in   **c.** is tired of

10. The woman describes herself as _____.

    a. a bargain-hunter   **b.** a comparison shopper   **c.** an impulse buyer

11. It is difficult for the woman to _____.

    a. splurge   **b.** resist temptation   **c.** go overboard

12. The man advises the woman to _____.

    a. go window-shopping   **b.** not go out   **c.** not carry credit cards

Complete each sentence by writing the words in parentheses in the correct order.

Example: Would you give me a few of those _big round sugar_ cookies?
        (round / sugar / big)

13. She opened the window and gazed out at the _____ sky.
        (morning / clear / blue)

14. In the shed, there were _____ motorcycles.
        (antique / British / two)

Circle the letter of the answer that correctly completes each sentence.

> **Example:** "Oh, what cute kittens! They're so _____!"
>
>   **a.** aggressive   **b.** costly   **c.** adorable

15. "I'd like a pet, but I don't have much spare time or money. Something _____ would be great."

    a. low maintenance   **b.** costly   **c.** good-natured

16. "I don't have any money, but I feel like going out. Do you want to go _____ downtown?"

    a. bargain-hunting   **b.** shopping   **c.** window-shopping

17. "Jill's parents always let her do anything she wanted. They were too _____ with her."

    a. lenient   **b.** overprotective   **c.** strict

18. "There are many stories about a lost city under the Atlantic, but with no evidence none are

    _____."

    a. questionable   **b.** unsolvable   **c.** provable

19. "I can't wait to try skydiving again. _____."

    a. It gets on my nerves   **b.** It scares the life out of me   **c.** There's nothing like it

20. "Have you ever tried _____ yoga?"

    a. doing   **b.** playing   **c.** making

21. "Do you _____ any hobbies?"

    a. do   **b.** have   **c.** practice

Complete each sentence by using the noun form of the correct verb or adjective from the box. You will not use all of the words.

fair	possible	difficult
explain	mobile	different
develop	~~attract~~	strict

> **Example:** "Sally's friends couldn't understand her _attraction_ to Mike, because they thought he was rude and vain."

22. "We never expected to have such _____ deciding what to do on the weekend."

23. "He always appreciated his parents' _____; they never treated one child better than the others."

24. "Historians don't have a good _____ for why the city was destroyed."

25. "I can't see much _____ between this dog and that one—they look almost exactly the same."

Complete each sentence with a phrase from the box. You will use one phrase more than once.

| might (not) be |
| should (not) be |
| must (not) be |
| (do not) have to be |

Example: "Parents of young children sometimes think that sweets and soft drinks _shouldn't be_ sold in schools."

26. "We are not advising, we are insisting: Cosmetics _____ tested on animals!"

27. "Maybe you should take your guitar this weekend; you _____ asked to play a few songs."

28. "Dolphins are so intelligent that some people believe they _____ trained to do sea rescues."

29. "Most animals _____ taught to swim; they can just do it naturally."

Complete each sentence by circling the correct word or phrase in parentheses and writing the correct form of be.

Example: "Writers (like/ can't stand) their books _to be_ read by lots of people."

30. "I'm very busy, and I **(resent / appreciate)** _____ bothered at home by people trying to sell me things."

31. "Mina was very unhappy. She didn't **(resent / appreciate)** _____ asked to clean up everyone else's mess."

Circle the letter of the answer that correctly completes each sentence.

Example: "People are waiting _____ to get married."

      a. long and long   **b.** long and longer   **c.** longer and longer

32. "The more I think about the exam, _____ nervous I feel."

      a. more   **b.** more and more   **c.** the more

33. "These stones _____ have been made by humans; there is no other explanation."

      a. might   **b.** should   **c.** must

34. "When Jason called Tuesday morning, he said the drawings _____ done by that afternoon."

      a. will be   **b.** would be   **c.** have to

35. "These footprints are very large. They _____ have been made by a bear or they could have been made by a lion."

      a. had to   **b.** couldn't   **c.** might

36. "A cure for that disease _____ be discovered through animal testing. We won't know if we don't try."

      a. could   **b.** must   **c.** can't

Complete each sentence in your own way. Use a double comparative.

Example: The bigger the car, *the more gasoline it uses*.

37. The larger the world's population grows, _____.

38. The better your education, _____.

39. The longer you live, _____.

Complete each sentence in your own way.

Example: I can't get enough of *going rock climbing*.

40. You'd have to be out of your mind to _____.

41. I can't wait to _____.

42. There's not a chance _____.

Read the fable. Then read it again and check <u>true</u> or <u>false</u>.

The Tortoise and the Eagle

Tortoise and Eagle had never met, as Eagle lived high in a tree and Tortoise lived on the ground. One day, however, Eagle heard how kind Tortoise was and decided to go visit him. Tortoise invited Eagle to stay for dinner. Eagle sat for several hours, eating the delicious food and admiring Tortoise's charming home. Eagle enjoyed the meal so much that he came back again and again. Each time he would eat as much as he could.

Eagle's visits made life hard for Tortoise. It was expensive to buy enough food to feed such a large bird. Also, Eagle was very messy, especially when eating. One day he even broke Tortoise's lamp and chair with his large, clumsy wings. It would take Tortoise a long time to clean up after each visit. However, Eagle didn't care about the difficulties he was causing. "Ha! I've eaten Tortoise's food, but he can never reach my tree to share mine!" he laughed proudly. One day Frog overheard this. He went to Tortoise and said, "You're too good-natured. Eagle is taking advantage of you." Then Frog told him what to do.

On Eagle's next visit, Tortoise said, "Please, friend, let me give you a pot of food to take home." Eagle accepted the gift and waited while Tortoise went into the kitchen. Tortoise hid inside a pot and called out, "Here's your food." Eagle grabbed the pot and flew to his home in the trees. But when he looked into the pot he was surprised to find only Tortoise. "Hello," said Tortoise. "I thought it'd be a nice change to visit your home. I look forward to sharing a meal with you."

Eagle became angry and said, "You will be the only meal here, Tortoise!" He tried to eat Tortoise but hurt his beak on Tortoise's hard shell. "I see what kind of friend you are, Eagle. Take me home," said Tortoise. "I'll drop you to the ground and smash you to pieces," screamed Eagle, and flew off with Tortoise in his claws. However, Tortoise grabbed onto Eagle's leg. "Please let go!" Eagle begged, trying to shake him off. "Only after you bring me home," Tortoise replied. Eagle had no choice but to comply. Once safely home, Tortoise turned and said, "A friend must be willing to give as well as receive. You're not welcome here anymore." Then he went inside, leaving Eagle to think about his selfishness.

Source: *The Tortoise and the Eagle* (traditional African fable)

	true	false
Example: The story is a fable about friendship.	☑	☐
43. Because Eagle was affectionate, he enjoyed visiting Tortoise.	☐	☐
44. Tortoise was generous to invite Eagle to eat dinner with him.	☐	☐
45. Eagle thought that Tortoise's home was charming.	☐	☐
46. Eagle was a low-maintenance guest.	☐	☐
47. Tortoise was mean to Eagle.	☐	☐
48. Preparing dinner for Eagle was costly.	☐	☐
49. Because of his large size, Eagle was destructive to Tortoise's furniture.	☐	☐
50. When Eagle laughed at Tortoise for giving him so many free meals, it showed that he was devoted.	☐	☐
51. Frog showed that he was gullible when he told Tortoise how to trick Eagle.	☐	☐
52. When Eagle discovered Tortoise in the pot, he became aggressive.	☐	☐
53. Tortoise was not being sincere when he said that a friend must give as well as receive.	☐	☐
54. Eagle cared only about himself and not about others.	☐	☐

Choose two of the following topics to write about. Write a paragraph of at least four to five sentences for each topic.

- In your opinion, should animals be kept in zoos or trained to perform in circuses?

- Some people buy on impulse while others shop around and bargain-hunt before making a purchase. What kind of shopper are you?

- Do you think family life has changed in any way in your lifetime? If so, how? Has the change been positive or negative?

- Describe an unsolved mystery, either a famous one or one from your own life. Explain what is known to have happened and what may or may not have happened.

- Agree or disagree with this statement: "Technology is making our lives easier and better by giving us more free time for hobbies and leisure activities." Talk about your own life and your own activities.

55–57. _____

_____

_____

_____

_____

58–60. _____

_____

_____

_____

_____

Name _____

Choose one of the following topics. On a separate sheet of paper, write an essay of at least three paragraphs. You will have 5 minutes to choose a topic and 30 minutes to write your essay.

Topic One

Why do you think people spend their free time reading books and watching movies about mysteries? Describe either a historical or fictional mystery from a book or movie you have read or watched. What unusual or unexpected things happen? Is the mystery solved? If not, speculate about what may or may not have happened. Why do you think people spend their time investigating this mystery?

Topic Two

Do you think the way that parents treat their teens affects the personalities that teens form? If parents are too strict, are they more likely to have rebellious teens? Is it wise for parents to be lenient with teens? Do you think parents' behavior relates to whether or not a teen will form a risk-taking personality? Give examples from your own life.

Name _____

Choose one of the following topics. Give a short talk of about 3 minutes to either your teacher or the whole class. You will have 5 minutes to prepare.

- How do you like to spend your free time? What are some of your hobbies and interests? Do you enjoy shopping? Do you have any pets that you enjoy spending time with?

- Compare your generation to your parents' generation. How do they differ? Have parent-teen issues changed? Do leisure activities vary from one generation to the next? Are there any general differences in attitudes toward shopping?

- Do you enjoy reading books or watching movies about mysteries in your free time? If so, why? What benefit do you get from these types of leisure activities? Describe one of your favorite mysteries.

UNIT 1

Conversation A

Carla: Dan, did you remember to make that invitation list for our New Year's party?

Dan: Oh, sorry, Carla. I've been putting in so many hours at the office. I just haven't had the time.

Carla: I know. You've been working so much recently. I hardly ever see you.

Dan: Well, I don't really have a choice. The boss gave me this big project to finish.

Carla: Your boss is always giving you big projects.

Dan: I know, but it's not just me—the guy's got everyone working hard.

Carla: Well, I hope you're not going to invite him to the party.

Dan: Definitely not.

Conversation B

Carla: What about the other guys at your office?

Dan: Actually, I was thinking of asking Harry. He's been helping me a lot this week—without him there's no way I'd ever get this project done.

Carla: Don't you think he'll feel a little uncomfortable? I mean, he won't know anyone at the party.

Dan: I doubt it—he's not the shy type. He loves meeting new people.

Carla: OK. So invite him. But hurry up with that list. I need to mail out the invitations tomorrow.

Conversation C

Dan: Hey, Carla. Here's that invitation list for the party.

Carla: Finally! Let's have a look. Hmm … You want to invite John?

Dan: Yeah, why not? He is our neighbor.

Carla: But he's such a pain in the neck! Last week he complained that our tree was dropping too many leaves in his yard.

Dan: Did he really?

Carla: And he thinks he's such a brain. I was outside replacing the porch light and he gave me this half-hour lecture on what type of light bulb to use.

Dan: Yeah, that's true. He thinks he has the answer to everything.

Carla: Then he made some dumb joke about how I was using the wrong tools. He's so annoying!

Dan: OK, you're right. Cross him off the list.

UNIT 2

Dennis: Sharon, how are you? I haven't seen you all week!

Sharon: Dennis! I'm fine, thanks, and you?

Dennis: Oh, all right. What have you been up to?

Sharon: Well, I saw a concert at the Omni last night. Theresa had an extra ticket and she invited me.

Dennis: Oh yeah? Who was playing?

Sharon: No one that I especially wanted to see—George Winston.

Dennis: George Winston … He's new age, right?

Sharon: Yeah, not really the kind of music I'm into …

Dennis: What was the show like?

Sharon: Well, you know that new age sound—happy, light, soothing. Lots of gentle keyboard melodies and mellow beats.

Dennis: That doesn't sound that bad to me, actually.

Sharon: It's OK, but I prefer something a little more exciting. I like to know what I've been listening to. New age is a little too much like background music to me.

Dennis: I don't know—sometimes I like to listen to relaxing music.

Sharon: I suppose, but it gets on my nerves a bit.

Dennis: What did Theresa think of it?

Sharon: Well, you know Theresa—she's really into new age music. And she actually loves George Winston. She's seen a lot of his shows, and she said that this one was the best yet.

Dennis: Well, at least one of you liked it. I'm almost afraid to ask you …

Sharon: What's that?

Dennis: I've got tickets to see Beyoncé next week—would you like to go?

Sharon: I'd love to! Now, that's more like it—something with a beat I can dance to!

UNIT 3

F: So, do you think about money much?

M: What do you mean? Doesn't everybody?

F: Well, for example, do you have any long-term financial goals?

M: Wow. Uh … Not really. I mostly think about getting the bills paid and whether or not I'll have enough left over to go out to a nice restaurant … like this one.

F: Sounds pretty short-term to me … If you sat down to make some plans now, what would they be?

M: OK … By this summer, I hope to have saved enough to take a trip somewhere …

F: Hmm … still short-term. I'm thinking of things like your career goals, or investing, or buying a house, or saving for retirement …

M: Had I known our date was going to be like this, I would have done some homework! Uh … No, to be honest, I never think about those things.

F: I do.

M: I can tell. OK, you go first—tell me about your goals.

F: Well, first I expect to have moved up to management by the time I'm 30.

M: OK—it could happen. What else?

F: Then I intend to have become a vice-president by 40.

M: Yes? Then what?

F: Well, by that time I plan to have bought a house and made enough investments that I'll be secure and won't have to work.

M: So you plan to retire at 40?

F: No, I think I'll keep working for awhile, but there won't be any pressure. I'll be able to quit whenever I want.

M: Sounds like you've given this a lot of thought.

F: Yes, I have. OK, your turn.

M: Right … Well, by the time I'm 40, I hope …

F: Go on …

M: I hope to have …

F: Yes?

M: I hope to have won a lot of money at a casino and retired to my yacht!

F: That's your long-term goal?

M: Yes. Now can we have dinner? I'll buy.

F: Well, thank you! Had I known you were buying, I'd have picked a more expensive restaurant.

UNIT 4

Margaret: Paul? Is that you?

Paul: Hey, Margaret!

Margaret: I almost didn't recognize you. Your hair! It's completely different!

Paul: I know. Do you like it?

Margaret: It's … um … interesting …

Paul: What do you really think?

Margaret: Well, it's a bit flashy.

Paul: A few of my friends have said that, but most of them seem to like it.

Margaret: I don't know—I guess I'll get used to it. Buzz cuts are trendy now … and, uh, … that bright red color is striking. But don't you think it might be shocking to some people? I mean after all, you work in a bank.

Paul: This color is in style—plenty of people have it. How shocking can it be?

Margaret: Hmm … I guess you're right. But what's your boss going to say? Fred's a pretty conservative guy.

Paul: Fred should be happy. He's the one who wanted me to get a haircut in the first place.

Margaret: Well, somehow, I don't think this is what he had in mind. Aren't you afraid that it's too flashy for work?

Paul: Do you really think so?

Margaret: Well, it would be different if you were a rock star or a fashion model. But you work in a bank—don't the majority of people there go for a more classic look?

Paul: Yes, but I wear a boring suit and tie every day, like I'm supposed to—I'd at least like to have a hot haircut.

Margaret: Well, no bank customers care about how stylish you are. They care about trust. With your job, you really don't need to be so trendy. Why not stick with a classic business look?

Paul: Hmm … Well, I'm going in to work tomorrow with this cut. If Fred says anything, I'll just go and have it all shaved off.

Margaret: I'm not sure the bald look will work either.

Paul: Why not? Fred's bald.

Margaret: Paul! Fred didn't shave his head. He's naturally bald.

Paul: But the customers don't know that.

Margaret: Well, do what you want. I'd hate to see you lose your job just because you want to be stylish.

UNIT 5

Matt: Hey, Sandra. What are you up to?

Sandra: Oh, hey, Matt. I'm just planning a trip to visit my grandparents in the country.

Matt: That's nice. It'll be nice to get away from the city for a few days, huh?

Sandra: Yeah … Hey, if you had a choice, would you ever consider living in the country?

Matt: Hmm … I never really thought about it before.

Sandra: I always think of you as a city boy.

Matt: Yeah, but I might like to try something different. Sometimes the city gets to me. I just can't understand the way people act here sometimes.

Sandra: What do you mean?

Matt: I don't know—the way they bump into you in crowds and then just walk away without even saying, "Excuse me." It's not their bumping into me that makes me angry—it's being ignored like that. It's so discourteous.

Sandra: You know, I hardly ever even notice that kind of stuff anymore.

Matt: Really? I do. Lately, it seems to be getting worse to me.

Sandra: Yeah? Well, people are pretty impolite, but that's just part of living in the city.

Matt: They're not only impolite, but they're also inconsiderate. They throw trash and cigarette butts around, they're always talking really loud on their cell phones … It really ticks me off.

Sandra: So, city boy, maybe you're really a country boy at heart.

Matt: I don't know though—I can't really see myself living in the country either. I'd miss all the great things there are to do in the city.

Sandra: Yeah, but if you had to choose?

Matt: Hmm … Maybe the suburbs …

Sandra: So the suburbs then, huh? How do you feel about shopping malls?

REVIEW TEST 1 (UNITS 1–5)

Listening A
Part 1

F: Good evening, ladies and gentlemen. It is with great pleasure that I welcome all of you to the sixth annual Community Service Awards. These awards recognize individuals who have made a special contribution to the lives of others.

Our first award, our Volunteer of the Year, goes to a real sweetheart, Mr. Michael Williams. For the past 25 summers, Mr. Williams has donated his time as a camp counselor at Camp Pine Lake, a non-profit camp that organizes outdoor activities for physically handicapped children. In that time, over 2,500 children have attended Camp Pine Lake, each of them with fond memories of the day they rode a horse for the first time, learned to swim, picked wildflowers, or sang campfire songs. And you can bet that Mr. Williams was by the side of each one of those kids, helping them to look past their handicaps and believe that they could do things well. In nominating Mr. Williams for this award, his fellow counselors were inspired not only by his talent for helping children, but his willingness to share his knowledge and experience with other staff members.

Part 2

F: Next, it's a great honor to present our second award, our Philanthropist of the Year, to Mrs. Eudora Wells, founder and president of Wells Industries. Two years ago, when a fire ripped through our downtown destroying our public library, our community was in need of help. Mrs. Wells decided to get involved. For most people, this would mean dropping a few dollars into a donation jar. But Mrs. Wells is not like most people. Already a dedicated supporter of reading programs at the library, Mrs. Wells decided on an unusual course of action—she donated all of the profits of her company to help rebuild the library. Not only that, but she worked hard to raise money from other corporate donors, eventually contributing over two million dollars. I'm delighted to report that in just two weeks, construction will begin on our beautiful new library—this just would not have been possible without Mrs. Wells's extraordinary gift.

Listening B

M1: Ugh … Why did I buy this thing? What a pain!

M2: What thing, Dad?

M1: This DVD player!

M2: DVD player? What's wrong with it?

M1: It gets about halfway through a DVD and then freezes. It just keeps blinking "disc error, disc error." But I can't find anything about a "disc error" in the manual.

M2: Could I see that? You're right, there's nothing in here about a "disc error."

M1: Had I known this thing was going to be so hard to operate, I would've kept the VCR.

M2: Well, you didn't know, Dad. Besides, it's getting harder and harder to find videotapes—especially for newer movies.

M1: It's so annoying! Just when you figure out one technology, they bring out a new one!

M2: So what are you going to do?

M1: I'm taking it back to the store. Maybe I can get another VCR.

M2: Dad, VCRs are so old-fashioned!

UNIT 6

M: Are you a dog person or a cat person?

F: Oh, I've always had dogs, ever since I was a kid.

M: Dogs? Or a dog?

F: Well, I only have one now, but I've had as many as three at one time.

M: Wow! Wasn't it hard to take care of them?

F: Not really. I mean, if you have big dogs they eat a lot of food, but …

M: What about walking them and all that?

F: You just take them all out together. And if you have more than one dog, they can keep each other company. They're not always begging for your attention.

M: That's funny, because I always thought dogs were kind of high maintenance. More than cats, anyway.

F: Yeah, maybe dogs need more attention than cats—for example, they definitely can't be left home alone for a long time. But I wouldn't exactly call them high maintenance.

M: Interesting … So what kind of dog do you have?

F: Now? A pit bull.

M: A pit bull? Aren't they aggressive?

F: Only if they're raised to be so. And I don't think animals should be trained to be aggressive—ever.

M: You must be really good with animals.

F: Oh, I don't know … I just seem to get along with them pretty well. I've had everything from poodles to shepherds, and they've all been pretty good-natured.

M: How about cats? Have you ever thought about getting a cat?

F: Cats are OK, but I don't know how Princess would feel about it.

M: Princess?

F: My pit bull.

M: Oh, right. So Princess doesn't like cats?

F: I'm not sure, but I don't really want to find out. So you're a cat person?

M: No, I don't actually have any pets right now. But I used to have an iguana.

F: And how was he? She?

M: Oh, she was great! Low maintenance and affectionate!

F: Seriously?

M: Oh, yeah, absolutely.

UNIT 7

Example

F: That store has great prices. I've never seen CDs for less than that.

M: You're kidding. I know a website where you can get them for much less.

F: Really? What is it? I'll check it out.

Conversation A

M: Can I help you find something?

F: No, thanks—I'm just looking.

M: Are you looking for anything special?

F: No, I'm just looking around.

Conversation B

F: How much are these socks?

M: Three pairs for five dollars.

F: Socks are only a dollar a pair across the street.

M: Yeah, and you know what? They're exactly the same socks that I'm selling. But they're a big store. I can't sell my products for as little as they can and still turn a profit. How about three pairs for four dollars?

F: Well, that's a surprise. I appreciate your honesty. It's a deal.

Conversation C

F: Look, they've got the new laptops on display.

M: Where?

F: Right there. In the window.

M: Should we be looking at new laptops right now? I thought we were trying to spend less.

F: Aww … I guess you're right. But look, you get a free MP3 player with your purchase if you buy before September 1st.

UNIT 8

Mark: Hey, Ellen. I ran into your baby sister the other day.

Ellen: Hi, Mark. You saw Janet? Where?

Mark: At the mall. She was with a bunch of friends. I didn't get a chance to talk to her. How's she doing?

Ellen: Pretty good. Going through a typical teenage phase … You know—wild clothes, talking back, acting up a little … nothing serious. She's actually a pretty good kid, even if she is a little spoiled. She'll shape up.

Mark: How much younger is Janet than you?

Ellen: Quite a bit. I was fifteen when she was born.

Mark: Wow. That's like two different generations. I didn't realize Janet was that much younger. Were your experiences really different?

Ellen: Yeah, for one thing, my parents were really strict with me. If I stayed out past my curfew, I got grounded. Even if I called ahead. No questions asked.

Mark: Really? What were they so worried about? You weren't rebellious or disrespectful, were you?

Ellen: No, not at all. But they were always worried. That made them overprotective. They always said, "Ellen, the rules are the rules. Period."

Mark: That sounds pretty extreme. What about with Janet? Are they that strict with her, too?

Ellen: No—just the opposite. They're ridiculously lenient with Janet. Listen to this. Just the other night, my sister was supposed to get home at eleven, and she didn't show up until 12:30.

Mark: Well, did she call to tell your parents she would be late?

Ellen: Are you kidding? That kid's always been rebellious. No way.

Mark: So what did your parents do? Ground her?

Ellen: No. They just gave her a warning. They said the next time she came home late, they'd take away her cell phone for a week. Can you imagine?

Mark: No wonder she's spoiled. It sounds like your parents have gotten pretty lenient in their old age—maybe a little too lenient. I just hope she doesn't turn out to be a troublemaker.

Ellen: I really doubt it. I think it's just a phase.

UNIT 9

F: I saw this interesting show last night on the Science Channel called "Man-made Mysteries."

M: Oh, yeah? How was it?

F: Well, one mystery really got me thinking. It was the mystery of the stone balls of Costa Rica.

M: Hmm … Never heard of them. What are they?

F: They're these stone balls, some small and some really big—like over 2 meters in diameter. Some weigh as much as 16 tons. They were discovered in the 1930s.

M: And they're sure they were man-made?

F: Yeah. The show said they were clearly man-made.

M: Hmm … I'm not an expert, but how could they know that the balls didn't occur naturally? What do they think they might have been used for?

F: The show didn't really say much about that.

M: Well, what do you think?

F: They might have been used as part of a big building. I don't know …

M: It's possible. Or they could have been used for some religious purpose.

F: Couldn't both explanations be true—they might have been part of a temple or church of some kind?

M: Maybe. Or maybe they were part of some big machine …

F: I don't think so … What kind of machine would have used stone balls of all different sizes? What would that machine have been used for?

M: I don't know, but it's an interesting idea.

F: Interesting, yes, but really questionable.

M: OK, not a machine, then. Hmm … The stones might have fallen from space …

F: And landed only in Costa Rica? That's really not believable.

M: Well, you've knocked down all my theories.

UNIT 10

Jeff: Hey, Gail. Long time no see. What's new?

Gail: Hi, Jeff. It has been a long time. What's new? Let me think … Well, one thing that's new is I've taken up karate. It's actually kind of changed my life.

Jeff: Karate? Hmm … Weren't you really into restoring antiques? And with that job of yours, how do you find the time for karate?

Gail: Well, I kind of burned out on the antiques. I couldn't keep all the furniture, and selling is really not my thing.

Jeff: But aren't antiques really hot right now? Could be pretty financially rewarding …

Gail: True. But I don't really need the money. I have a good job. I was getting really out of shape, so I started looking for something a little more physically challenging. No pain, no gain—you know?

Jeff: Hmm …

Gail: Turns out that karate really fits the bill. I absolutely can't get enough of it. In fact, I'm on my way to a class right now.

Jeff: Well, they say martial arts are great for getting in shape. How long have you been doing karate?

Gail: Only about two months. But it's paying off already. Just look at this muscle!

Jeff: Not bad.

Gail: Thanks. Hey, didn't you use to do karate or tae kwon do or something like that?

Jeff: Actually no, yoga. I'm a yoga freak. It's hard to believe, but they say it's just as challenging as karate, but more spiritual—it really calms me down and helps me get in touch with my emotions, if you know what I mean.

Gail: You know, I find karate spiritually and emotionally satisfying as well. It's not all about kicking and fighting, even though it's a martial art. And for me, it's a nice social outlet. I've made a lot of friends at the center. It's a really great group of people. One of the things I didn't like about the antiques was that I spent too much time alone.

REVIEW TEST 2 (UNITS 6–10)

Listening A

M: Parents: Do you worry that your kids are getting spoiled? Let's face it, no matter how strict you try to be, kids today are getting more and more rebellious and disrespectful with each passing day. There is something you can do: Send them to us at Miyazawa Karate Dojo for our special three-month intensive children's course. We will train them in the skills and discipline of the ancient martial art of karate. Your kids will be able to work out their aggressive feelings in a safe, supervised environment. They will learn and grow, not only physically, but emotionally and spiritually as well. They will learn both obedience and independence. Help your children take giant steps toward maturity. Come and visit us today at Miyazawa Karate Dojo.

Listening B

F: I've got to do something about my spending. I'm turning into a spendthrift.

M: What's wrong with that? People have to buy things, or the economy will go down the tubes.

F: Well, I know that, but I think I'm kind of getting out of control financially. I just got my credit card bill, and it's pretty scary.

M: How bad is it?

F: Well, I'm not ruined—not yet, anyway. But if I go overboard every month like this, I'm just going to get deeper and deeper in debt.

M: That's rough. Have you ever tried being a little stricter with yourself, like making a budget and sticking to it?

F: That doesn't work for me. Once I get the urge, I don't seem to be able to resist. I start out with window-shopping, and the next thing you know, I'm buying everything in the store.

M: Hmm … Try this: When you go out, don't take your credit cards. And only take a little bit of cash. The less you carry, the less you can spend.

F: OK, I'll try it. It might work.

M: Don't say "might." It'll work if you stick to it. It's up to you. You have to be strong.

F: Strong! OK!

■ Answer Key

Note: *"Sample response" indicates a sample of what students may produce. Answers will vary. Sample responses throughout the tests do not necessarily indicate the "correct" response.*

UNIT 1

1. true
2. true
3. true
4. false
5. false
6. true
7. workaholic
8. people person
9. brain
10. positive
11. positive
12. negative
13. negative
14. to ask
15. hearing
16. to like
17. meeting
18. to take
19. to eat
20. seeing
21. asking
22. Lilyflower thinks her boss is a tyrant.
23. Fox223's new boss is a sweetheart.
24. Fox223's new boss is a people person.
25. Fox223 is a team player.
26. Lil'Marie fears that Lilyflower is a workaholic.
27. Lil'Marie thinks that Lilyflower's boss makers her work extremely hard.
28. *(Sample response:)* friend; sweetheart; She is always so easy to get along with.
29. *(Sample response:)* brother; workaholic; He is always working and never does anything else.
30. *(Sample response:)* boss; tyrant; He makes us work extremely hard all the time.
31–33. *(Sample response:)* There are pros and cons to both optimism and pessimism. Optimists tend to be very hopeful and always expect the best results. This perspective can be uplifting and inspiring; however, it is not always realistic. Pessimists, on the other hand, tend to be more cynical and focus on the problems of a given situation. While it is important to recognize and acknowledge difficulties, this perspective can make people want to give up. Being flexible enough to be able to go back and forth between these two perspectives in different situations is essential.

(Sample response:) For me, finding balance in life can be quite challenging at times. I often over-schedule myself and find that I have no time for myself and not enough time for my family and friends. Some of my friends say that I am a workaholic, but the truth is just that my boss can be a real tyrant. They say I need to stop worrying about work so much and remember to enjoy life more. I know that they are right and plan to remember to make more time for the important people in my life from now on.

UNIT 2

1. is passionate about
2. boring
3. Beyoncé's
4. excited
5. Theresa
6. Dennis
7. b
8. c
9. a
10. a
11. c
12. annoyed; annoying
13. depressed; depressing
14. boring; bored
15. exciting; excited
16. false
17. false
18. true
19. true
20. false
21. true
22. true
23. has been playing
24. have you seen
25. bought
26. have been practicing
27. Have you heard
28. *(Sample response:)* that I can share my passion for music with others
29. *(Sample response:)* what she should wear tonight
30. *(Sample response:)* that music brings joy to people and enriches their lives
31–33. *(Sample response:)* My favorite type of music is jazz. I love the loud, rhythmic beats common to it. I particularly enjoy listening to live performances where musicians often spontaneously create new melodies and often blend two or more melodies together. I also like listening to jazz at home while studying because with so few lyrics, it is the perfect background music.

(Sample response:) My cousin, Marie, is the most musically talented person I know. She is in a band that has performed all around the world. She plays the guitar and the piano and has an absolutely beautiful voice. Everyone in our family always knew that Marie would be successful because she has always been so passionate about music and is such amazingly gifted person.

UNIT 3

1. true
2. true
3. false
4. false
5. true
6. false
7. a
8. b
9. c
10. c
11. a
12. charity
13. contribution
14. profit
15. Had I known this furniture would be so hard to put together, I wouldn't have bought it.
16. Had we realized this couch wouldn't fit in the elevator, we would've bought a smaller one.
17. Had he known that his digital camera would just sit around collecting dust, he wouldn't have bought such an expensive one.

18. *(Sample response:)* finish school; to have saved up enough money to be able to buy a car
19. *(Sample response:)* to have paid off all my credit card debt
20. *(Sample response:)* will have saved enough money to be able to retire
21. buy gifts
22. buyer's remorse
23. cost too much to maintain
24. take up so much room
25. operate
26. put together
27. just sits around collecting dust
28. c
29. b
30. a
31–33. *(Sample response:)* My financial goal for the next year is to save enough money to be able to go on a trip to Japan. First, I plan to cut back on my spending as much as possible. I will not buy any new clothes and won't eat out at any expensive restaurants. Next, I intend to invest the money that I save so that it will grow faster. I hope to have enough money saved by winter.

(Sample response:) I have donated money to many different charities. I try to only contribute to organizations that are well-known and reputable, such as the Red Cross, so that I know my money will be used well. I plan to continue to donate money to this and other non-profit organizations and hope to be able to afford to give even more in the future. I also enjoy giving to local fundraisers such as those held for the schools in my community and I intend to be as generous as possible to them in the future as well.

UNIT 4

1. A few of Paul's friends think his haircut is too flashy.
2. Margaret thinks buzz cuts are hot right now.
3. Margaret thinks Paul's hair color might be offensive to some people.
4. Margaret thinks most bank employees dress in a classic way.
5. Paul wears formal business clothes to work.

6. Margaret thinks most bank customers don't trust bank employees who dress in a shocking way.
7. image
8. conscious
9. esteem
10. pity
11. b
12. a
13. c
14. a
15. b
16. a
17. b
18. a
19. b
20. c
21. *(Sample response:)* employees enjoy casual Fridays
22. *(Sample response:)* of the time, I wear jeans to school
23. *(Sample response:)* of my friends wear contact lenses
24. a little
25. The majority
26. less
27. most
28. Many
29. a great deal of
30. Only a few
31–33. *(Sample response:)* The clothes I wear at work, at home, and when I'm out with my friends are all very different. When I'm at work, I wear business casual clothes. I always try to look professional. When I'm out with my friends, I enjoy wearing my more fashionable, trendy clothes and love not having to worry about any dress codes. At home, however, my first priority for clothes is comfort! I have no concern for fashion at all when I'm at home just relaxing.

(Sample response:) I prefer a classic look to a trendy one. Whereas many of my friends buy a lot of flashy clothes they wear only a few times, I choose to buy clothes that I know I will always love. Like my friends, I don't mind spending a lot of money on clothes. However, I only buy clothes that I know will be timeless. Some of my friends like to constantly change their entire wardrobes, but I prefer to update mine slowly and to be more selective with what I buy.

UNIT 5

1. true
2. false
3. true
4. true
5. false
6. unacceptable
7. improper
8. dishonest
9. inexcusable
10. irrational
11. volunteers
12. donating your organs
13. clean up litter
14. *(Sample response:)* My roommate's playing loud music while I'm sleeping
15. *(Sample response:)* Mary's talking on her cell phone while she's driving really
16. *(Sample response:)* His telling everyone what to do all the time
17. Jacob says that his moving out of the city is the best thing he has ever done for himself.
18. Maria's boyfriend is getting worried about her smoking.
19. I think their arguing is getting worse and worse.
20. Chris's boss is really getting annoyed by his talking on his cell phone during meetings.
21. Driving in the city is neither convenient nor enjoyable.
22. You can help your community by either volunteering your time or donating money.
23. Smoke-filled rooms are not only unpleasant but also unhealthy.
24. Not only was the traffic terrible, but the weather was also awful.
25. a
26. b
27. c
28. a
29. b
30. c
31–33. *(Sample response:)* It really bugs me when people talk on their cell phones on the train. When others are trying to sleep or read, their talking loudly is so inconsiderate. I can understand their making important calls, but I shouldn't have to listen to people talk about what they want for dinner. People who just keep talking even though they're obviously disturbing others around them are either

completely oblivious or just self-centered.

(Sample response:) I think unemployment, pollution, and corruption are the most serious urban problems today. Being unable to find work makes life extremely difficult for individuals and for families. Wide-scale unemployment can lead to other urban problems such as crime and poverty. Pollution is a very serious problem because damage to the environment can be irreversible. Finally, corruption in government is often the cause of these as well as other urban problems.

REVIEW TEST 1

1. b
2. a
3. b
4. b
5. a
6. b
7. c
8. c
9. c
10. b
11. a
12. a
13. b
14. a
15. b
16. c
17. b
18. c
19. a
20. a
21. b
22. self-conscious
23. inappropriate
24. unimaginable
25. dishonest
26. irrational
27. to write
28. to turn
29. asking
30. have been practicing
31. have been performing
32. saw
33. a
34. b
35. b
36. (Sample response:) I don't mind his listening to music all the time while he's working.

37. (Sample response:) I really like their dressing in casual attire on Fridays.
38. (Sample response:) I really don't appreciate his talking on the phone to friends while he's at work.
39. (Sample response:) get married; have already bought my first house
40. (Sample response:) to have saved enough money to buy a new car
41. (Sample response:) I finish school; be able to get a good job
42. true
43. false
44. false
45. true
46. false
47. false
48. false
49. false
50. true
51. true
52. true
53. false
54. false
55–57. / 58–60.

(Sample response:) My brother's personality has completely changed. When we were growing up, he was such a wise guy. He was always making dumb jokes that really got on my nerves; he could be so difficult. As we got older, however, he started to become more mature and learned to stop annoying people so much. Now, most people actually think of him as a sweetheart!

(Sample response:) My favorite singer is Sarah McLachlan. She is an extremely gifted and talented musician. Her voice is absolutely beautiful and her lyrics are passionate and touching. She is very creative and her albums have a great variety of beats and sounds. She has so many great songs.

(Sample response:) I plan to open a restaurant of my own by this time next year. First, I intend to have saved enough money to open the restaurant by the summer. Once I have enough money saved, I'll begin hiring my staff, including a great chef. Finally, I plan to decorate the restaurant in an

elegant, chic style. I hope that it will be a great success.

(Sample response:) When I was growing up in the 1980s, fashion was much different than it is today. Really tight pants, big sweatshirts, and bright, flashy colors were all very trendy then. In terms of hair, almost all women used a lot of hair spray to make their hair look as big as possible. They also wore a lot of bright makeup, such as blue eye shadow. By today's standards these looks are considered tacky and are very much out of style.

(Sample response:) One problem in my town is inadequate public transportation. The only public transportation in my town is a bus service that runs too infrequently. Also, the bus makes so many stops and has such a long, winding route that it takes twice as long to get from one side of town to the other by bus than by car. For these reasons, people rely on their cars and hardly ever use the bus service. I think that our local government should either put more money into providing a better bus service or build a subway system. If the public transportation were improved, more people would pay to use it.

UNIT 6

1. true
2. false
3. false
4. false
5. false
6. true
7. aggressive
8. adorable
9. filthy
10. destructive
11. costly
12. c
13. a
14. b
15. a
16. should be tested
17. could be used
18. might not be given
19. has to be stopped
20. have to be used

21. (Sample response:) Animals don't have to be killed for their hides or fur; it's not necessary.
22. (Sample response:) Animals should be trained to help people with disabilities.
23. (Sample response:) Animals shouldn't be kept in zoos that are too small or otherwise inappropriate for them.
24. a
25. c
26. a
27. c
28. a
29. c
30. c
31–33. (Sample response:) While it may seem cruel to some, animals must be used for medical research. Without the use of animals, new vaccines might not be discovered. Maybe one day we will have the technology to test various medicines without using animals. As of now, however, animals have to be used in order to protect human life. There is no other way.

(Sample response:) My favorite pet was my cat, Whiskers. Whiskers was an extremely affectionate and good-natured cat. He was very loyal and devoted to us and to our other cats. In some ways, he had more the personality of a dog than a cat. In fact, he used to try to follow us around everywhere we went—it was so cute!

UNIT 7

1. a
2. c
3. c
4. b
5. b
6. a
7. window-shop
8. haggle
9. bargain-hunt
10. shop around
11. browse
12. blows me away
13. cracked me up
14. choke me up
15. gets on my nerves
16. to be remembered
17. being entertained
18. to be told

19. being treated
20. not to be asked
21. (Sample response:) to be given much help with the cleaning
22. (Sample response:) being told what to do all the time
23. (Sample response:) being asked about our time traveling through Europe
24. comparison shop
25. informed
26. steal from you
27. several things
28. a bit steep
29. implies
30. find great offers
31–33. (Sample response:) My best friend, Camille, is a compulsive shopper. When Camille sees something she likes in a store, she just cannot resist the temptation to buy it right away. Not only that, but when she is not in a store or mall, she often wishes she were and gets the urge to go shopping. She indulges herself and goes shopping almost every day. Of course, she has a big problem with overspending.

(Sample response:) One impulse buy that I regret making is my large-screen TV. I enjoy being entertained in style in my own house and I had been resisting the urge to splurge on something for a few weeks when I finally broke down and bought it. However, I definitely went overboard—talk about overspending! I didn't expect to be ruined financially for the sake of a TV, but I came close! I think next time I'll resist such temptations.

UNIT 8

1. Ellen
2. differently
3. lenient
4. well-behaved
5. disrespectful
6. overprotective
7. a little spoiled
8. happiness
9. expectation
10. responsibility
11. development
12. importance

13. Life expectancy is getting higher and higher.
14. Divorce is becoming more and more common.
15. People are working longer and longer hours now.
16. Health care is getting better and better.
17. The longer people live, the more care they require.
18. The better health care gets, the higher life expectancy gets/becomes.
19. The higher life expectancy gets, the larger the elderly population gets/becomes.
20. The harder people work, the more successful they are/become.
21. (Sample response:) expect to get/have or do whatever they want; always ask their parents to buy them expensive things
22. (Sample response:) worry too much about their kids; have too many rules
23. (Sample response:) let their kids have or do anything they want; don't have any rules
24. b
25. c
26. a
27. a
28. b
29. c
30. b
31–33. (Sample response:) Families today are getting smaller and smaller. People are having fewer and fewer children. This has both positive and negative effects on families. When parents have fewer children, they are able to give more attention to each child they have. However, the more common only children become, the fewer brothers, sisters, aunts, uncles, and cousins there will be.

(Sample response:) My generation is very different from my parents' generation. Their generation was more laid back and easygoing than mine is today. My generation is generally serious and career-minded. The job market now is a lot more competitive than it used to be and the cost of living is much higher, so my generation has to be more focused just to achieve the same things our parents did.

■ **Answer Key (continued)**

UNIT 9

1. c
2. a
3. c
4. a
5. b
6. a
7. not certain
8. not certain
9. certain
10. *(Sample response:)* I'll bet they switched classrooms at the last minute.
11. *(Sample response:)* I suppose Jack could have gone over to his neighbor's apartment for a little while.
12. *(Sample response:)* I guess they must have fallen out of your pocket.
13. unsolvable
14. debatable
15. provable
16. would
17. might
18. would
19. might
20. should
21. true
22. false
23. true
24. false
25. false
26. true
27. a
28. a
29. c
30. b
31–33. *(Sample response:)* The Bermuda Triangle is an area of the Atlantic Ocean between Bermuda, Florida, and Puerto Rico. There have been many disappearances of ships in this area. No one knows what may have happened to the ships that passed through this area because they disappeared without a trace. Some people think these disappearances had to have been caused by the sudden thunderstorms that are common in that area. Others think they might have been caused by the high waves and strong currents that are also common there.

UNIT 10

1. c
2. a
3. a
4. b
5. b
6. c
7. c
8. f
9. a
10. d
11. b
12. beautiful French silk
13. nice young Chinese
14. some interesting history
15. huge round glass
16. one thousand rare old
17. physically
18. financially
19. socially
20. emotionally
21. intellectually
22. *(Sample response:)* I can't wait to go surfing.
23. *(Sample response:)* White-water rafting scares the life out of me.
24. *(Sample response:)* Hang gliding doesn't scare me a bit.
25. true
26. true
27. false
28. true
29. false
30. false
31–33. *(Sample response:)* My favorite leisure activity is playing chess. I find chess very intellectually stimulating and challenging. I enjoy playing with my friends and family. I probably spend more time with them because we enjoy playing chess so much, so it is socially satisfying as well. There's nothing like a great game of chess!

(Sample response:) I definitely enjoy taking risks and have a risk-taking personality. I get bored easily and crave adventure. I can't get enough of extreme sports such as surfing or downhill skiing. There's nothing like the rush you get when flying down an icy mountainside or the thrill riding a gigantic wave.

REVIEW TEST 2

1. c
2. b
3. c
4. c
5. a
6. b
7. c
8. b
9. a
10. c
11. b
12. c
13. clear blue morning
14. two antique British
15. a
16. c
17. a
18. c
19. c
20. a
21. b
22. difficulty
23. fairness
24. explanation
25. difference
26. must not be
27. might be
28. should be
29. do not have to be
30. resent; being
31. appreciate; being
32. c
33. c
34. b
35. c
36. a
37. *(Sample response:)* the more natural resources will be needed
38. *(Sample response:)* the more likely you are to succeed
39. *(Sample response:)* the more care you will need
40. *(Sample response:)* go skydiving
41. *(Sample response:)* go downhill skiing
42. *(Sample response:)* I'd ever go bungee jumping
43. false
44. true
45. true
46. false
47. false
48. true
49. true
50. false
51. false
52. true
53. false
54. true

■ **Answer Key (continued)**

55–57. / 58 –60.

(Sample response:) In my opinion, animals should not be kept in zoos or trained to perform in circuses. In both of these cases, animals are treated cruelly simply for our entertainment. Animals should be allowed to be free and shouldn't be forced to live out their lives in cages just so that zoos and circuses can make money. If people really want to see and learn about animals, they could either watch documentaries about them on TV or they could go on safaris where they could observe animals in their natural environments.

(Sample response:) I am definitely a bargain-hunter. I never make purchases on impulse. In fact, I often make several trips to a store or stores before buying something. I always look for coupons and wait for sales. My one weakness is if I find something that I think is a steal, I'll buy it even if I don't need it—or even like it that much—just because it's a great offer.

(Sample response:) In my lifetime, family life has changed gradually. In general, people seem to be marrying and having children later and later in life now. I think this change is positive because people are waiting until they are more prepared to have children. The more prepared people are, the better parents they will be.

(Sample response:) One mystery that I've always found fascinating is that of the Nazca Lines in Peru. It's amazing that people could have carved these lines, which form a design when viewed from the air, into the earth more than 1500 years ago without the use of airplanes. No one knows how these designs were made. Some people think the lines may have been created by aliens. Others think the lines must not have actually been carved until about 1927, after airplanes had been invented.

(Sample response:) I think that technology does make our lives easier and better in many ways. There are certainly many devices that allow us to get more done faster than we could before. However, as our ability to get more done increases, so do our expectations for how much we should be getting done. Therefore, just because technology may enable us to get work done faster doesn't mean that we have more free time.

■ Summit 1

Complete Assessment Package Audio CD Tracking Guide

Track	Listening
1	Program Introduction
2	Unit 1 Achievement Test
3	Unit 2 Achievement Test
4	Unit 3 Achievement Test
5	Unit 4 Achievement Test
6	Unit 5 Achievement Test
7	Units 1–5 Review Test 1
8	Unit 6 Achievement Test
9	Unit 7 Achievement Test
10	Unit 8 Achievement Test
11	Unit 9 Achievement Test
12	Unit 10 Achievement Test
13	Units 6–10 Review Test 2